Many Cells
One Body

Ian M. Fraser

Many Cells
One Body

Stories from Small
Christian Communities

Risk
BOOK SERIES

WCC Publications, Geneva

Cover design: Rob Lucas

ISBN 2-8254-1370-4

© 2003, WCC Publications, World Council of Churches
P.O. Box 2100, 150 route de Ferney
1211 Geneva 2, Switzerland

Website: http://www.wcc-coe.org

No. 101 in the Risk Book Series

Printed in Switzerland

Table of Contents

For
Allison and Mike
Sonaly and Chuck

and with appreciation to
Leslie Cram and Bob Marshall
for their processing work

Foreword

Lord God,
whose Son was content to die
to bring new life,
have mercy on your church,
which will do anything you ask,
anything at all,
except die and be reborn.

Lord Christ,
forbid us unity
which leaves us where we are
and as we are:
welded into one company
but extracted from the battle;
engaged to be yours,
but not found at your side.

Holy Spirit of God,
reach deeper than our inertia and fears:
release us into the freedom of children of God.

Amen.

A phenomenon of our time is the growth of Small Christian Communities (SCCs). These have been called, in earlier years, Christian Grassroots Communities (CGCs), Basic Christian Communities (BCCs) or Basic Ecclesial Communities (BECs). In China, they are "house churches", in Australia "home churches". The term most often used now is Small Christian Communities or SCCs. In the interviews which follow, I retain the designation used by the person being interviewed.

My own involvement dates back to 1941 when I became a member of the Iona community in Scotland. Through the 1940s, we hammered out a discipline designed to keep us faithful to a commitment to live the Christian faith with fresh imagination and to be accountable to one another in doing so. That provided priorities which, I believe, could be affirmed today by SCCs all over the world. About 1950, we moved into groupings according to our geographical locations (at present there are thirty of these in Britain). These "family groups" fed into and heard reports from three plenaries each year and were gathered into an annual community week on the island of Iona. I see these as early "John the Baptist" signs of the world development to come.

Since then, over the decades, there have been particular points at which I have established additional relationships with SCCs in different parts of the world (to date I have been in 95 countries). I have recorded interviews on tape so that the emphases and nuances of different life-styles might be retained. Where a language was unknown (and there are over seventy indigenous languages in the Philippines alone!), the SCCs were asked to appoint an interpreter whom they could trust. Interviews with over three hundred SCCs on every continent can now be consulted in the Baker Library in Scottish Churches House, Dunblane.

An extension of contacts came with my appointment in 1969 to the staff of the World Council of Churches with responsibility for one of the five major programmes approved at the 1968 Uppsala assembly and entitled "Participation in Change". To me, it was clear that this programme should be directed to the world's poor. How were the poor coping with the drastic changes that put such severe pressure on their lives? What resource had the Christian faith proved to be to them? Immediately, my travels brought me into contact with SCCs. They proved to be the bearers of life and hope to people in desperate situations. I encountered SCCs in the shanty-towns and in the heart of big cities as a form of church in which the poor were no longer alienated but knew that God's purpose embraced them as and where they were. My report to the WCC's Nairobi assembly in 1975, entitled "The Fire Runs", was full of their stories.

Meanwhile, I had been asked to set up a department of mission in Selly Oak Colleges, Birmingham, England and act as dean to coordinate the work of the relevant colleges. At first, I thought that with this new appointment I could leave behind me the networking with SCCs. But I soon came to realize that the main signs of fresh and sensitive missionary outreach in our time were those seen in the life of SCCs. The

1968 Medellín conference had spoken of the small ecclesial community as "the cell of the church and the radiating centre for its evangelizing efforts". So I extended and enlarged contacts with these "radiating" centres.

When the time came to retire, the British missionary societies and boards asked my wife Margaret and myself to fulfil a joint mandate, at first over a two-year period and then, if the project proved fruitful, over a further three years. We were to spend six weeks with SCCs in the north, centre and south of the Philippines (which I had visited previously but Margaret had not), visit or revisit those in Eastern and Western Europe, and finally bring back insights provided by SCCs for the renewal of the church in our time. Margaret died in 1987 after four and a half years of memorable partnership in this work. I have continued, and I hope that this book will go some way to fulfil that joint mandate.

At San Martin, about 70 kilometres from Barcelona, where the Barcelona area SCCs were holding a weekend of retreat and reappraisal, Fr Juan Garcia Nieto accosted me with a twinkle in his eye: "What do you think the people here are calling you?"

"I haven't a clue."

"They're calling you a prophet."

"Why?"

"Well, in the early days of the church, prophets moved around among the small communities, conveyed news, made creative links between them. They see you in that role."

He added, the twinkle becoming twinklier:

"Then they say, 'But why someone from Scotland? Why Scotland?'"

Paul had the only possible answer: "The folly of God is wiser than human wisdom." All kinds are drafted for unlikely tasks!

The first part of this book is intended to get across a sense of the life-styles of SCCs, in so far as I have been able to share their joys and hopes and struggles. These stories, while they come from the 1960s, reveal life-styles which are just as telling and vibrant today. The circumstances from which they arise differ widely. The same Spirit is at work.

The second part of the book looks at traditional marks of the church to see how SCCs stand up to these criteria. The final part is a look forward.

1. This Surge of Life

Small Christian communities: what explains this surge of new life-in-community in the 20th century?

Strong contributory elements were the founding of the World Council of Churches (WCC) and the work of the Second Vatican Council.

From early days the WCC laid emphasis on the laity as the body not so much called to "attend church" but to "be church" and to "live church". At the New Delhi assembly of the WCC in 1961, the ministry of the laity was a central issue in section discussions. During the Second Vatican Council, Pope John XXIII invited the World Council to appoint 15 people, Orthodox, Reformed and Lutheran, to meet informally with an equal of number of Catholics on the topic "The Church in the Modern World"; the group, which I chaired twice, met three times prior to the laity congress in 1967. WCC work on laity then merged with the "Participation in Change" programme. Meanwhile, Vatican II had changed the emphasis on the understanding of church from that placed on hierarchy in 1870 at Vatican I to "the people of God".

All this had a liberating effect on ordinary church members, especially Roman Catholics, examples of whose SCCs are used disproportionately hereafter, since they had a hierarchy, often traditionalist, to contend with. This added a sharper edge to Catholic perceptions of what essentially belongs to faith. For all that, small Christian communities are essentially ecumenical.

Take-off points

The take-off points which led to the creation of SCCs involved a variety of circumstances. Was this not characteristic of the Corinthian church which, among many other areas of difference, boasted Paulites, Apollosites, Cephasites and Christites (1 Cor. 1:12)? In an interview I conducted in Guatemala, it was observed:

> It is in the very nature of Christian communities that every community has its own special character. They are not clones. The seven hundred groups in the Waiwaitenango area are of seven

hundred different kinds. So it would be very difficult to say that there is a model or type which you could label as standard.

The responder went on to say that in areas where there was Indian indigenous culture, a basic homogeneity existed. In all this variety, the Holy Spirit provided a unity of life and witness.

The incentive to form SCCs may come from some official trend or simply from concrete local circumstances.

During Vatican II, the Italian bishops voted substantially against progressive measures – and were outvoted. When the riots, revolts and near revolutions of 1968 took place, they saw their chance and argued in favour of restoration. Everything was sliding into chaos. The disciplines of the old order had to be reasserted. At this point, there was a surge in the development of SCCs on the part of people who resisted this reactionary move. They were simply saying, "We are going on with Vatican II."

In Czechoslovakia and Hungary, the spur was the communist occupation. Some church leaders collaborated with the communists. Other Christians started to meet clandestinely in small communities out of the sight of the secret police. It was only when the Velvet Revolution took place two decades later that they could link up with one another as people with different Christian backgrounds who had been inspired and strengthened by the one Spirit.

In China, a woman, a product of Mao's atheism, might take note of a change in a neighbour who seemed to be living with new zest and purpose. She would keep an eye on the neighbour for some time and then would find a natural opportunity to question her. "You seem different. Have you won the lottery?" she might ask. And she would be told of the neighbour's encounter with Jesus Christ. She would be invited, not to a congregational gathering at that point, but to a house church which would be small enough to allow her to relate with ease to others and feel that she could go deeper into this faith which had transforming power.

The local trigger might be a situation revealing the weakness and unfaithfulness of the official church. This was the case in the Basque country. A layman responded this way to the question of how the SCCs in that area got going:

> It was with an event – the event of 3 March 1976. There was a strike which went on for a month and involved the whole factory population of this area. Trade union activity was forbidden. But the workers got access to a church. The police threw in smoke bombs. When the people came out, five were killed by police fire. That was the impulse which really led to the development of Basic Christian Communities (BCCs) here. The bishop in the area did not respond in any Christian way to the killing of workmen, so those who had been angered by this event made up their mind they had to discover for themselves what the faith had to say to them. Those concerned – quite a mixture of people – got together to develop the structures of pressure for justice. The fact that they were not acting merely politically, but from the point of view of faith, was something new and raised questions. The initiative was essentially lay. Although there were those in the official church who were sympathetic and supportive, the main authorities of the church did not become involved.
>
> This movement had to take place outside the parishes which were lined up with the church hierarchy. To start with, all the groups had a priest attached to act as a coordinator and to be, in a certain way, a specialist in faith. Essentially, the BCCs analyzed the situation and then tried to work out what the Christian response should be. This process led to other, much wider, questions about life. These had not been opened to them before. There was no intention of putting a distance between themselves and the official church – they simply were the church trying to live its life faithfully. Questions of divorce, abortion, the media and violence became matters that people no longer left to the authorities but tried to make sense of themselves. The official church tried to call this movement a parallel church, whereas it was simply church. The gospel is more likely to make us fear the temptations of power than the possibilities of revolution!

I was in Guatemala and El Salvador when they were killing fields. I asked what impelled poor people, in the face of hostility of authorities, to risk their lives in forming SCCs. I was given the following answer:

What's happening, I believe, is that the Indians and other rural people are becoming aware of their Christian responsibilities and are growing to Christian maturity. They realize that they have a job to do as Christians here in the world. The fact that they protest their poverty, and the fact that they are now recognizing that this gruesome life which kills off their children is not the will of God, is being seen as a threat to the whole status quo of the country. Basic Christian communities are an anathema to the people who don't want to see the status quo changed.

Was there a tendency for the powers that be, then, to identify the leaders of BCCs and try to get rid of them? Were they suffering particularly?

In the international press, you'll hear about the priests and sisters who are being massacred here in Guatemala, but you rarely ever hear of the catechists who have disappeared – and most of the catechists are leaders of the BCCs. I don't think we could even begin to count the number of catechists who have had to pay the supreme sacrifice. But the fact that they have given their lives is, to me, a sign that they have become fully aware of their own Christian identities and their own role as leaders within the Christian community.

Under the Marcos dictatorship in the Philippines, SCCs were seen as possible hotbeds of subversion. What brought them into being was indeed a demand for justice. In my notes of a visit in 1982, I record the following:

Margaret and I had spent most of the evening before his arrest with Fr Brian Gore, an Australian priest. The next day he went to Bacolod. There the military tried to seize him but the bishop of the area – Bishop Fortich – showed great courage and insisted that he would deliver his priest to the military centre in Kabankalan with dignity. Bishop and priest returned to Kabankalan with lay workers who were also to be arrested. We joined hundreds of people who, singing hymns defiantly, walked with them to where soldiers in military carriers, guns at the ready, ringed the centre where the hand-over took place. The charge related to bullets and a grenade allegedly found in Brian Gore's room. "It must have been a rubber grenade," said Bishop Fortich. "The first report said that it was found in a drawer of a filing cabinet, the next that it was on top. It must have bounced!"

The trial dragged on. Eventually, the charges were shown to be fabrications. We knew the real reason for the arrest. In conversation the previous evening, Brian Gore had told us of the BCCs which had developed in the mountains and the nearby plain, and how a poor, malnourished people had learned to form cooperatives to gain a more adequate return for their labour. The Bible was now in their hands and was a source of life. They met in it a God who set his face against injustices such as they had experienced. Nothing is more unwelcome to those wielding power unjustly than awakened, thinking human beings!

The take-off point in some regions might be the need to overcome alienation by forming community.

A school porter from Barcelona commented on the difference it makes if there is an SCC to which one may turn when people move from a familiar background to a strange part of their own country:

> What is it like to be an immigrant, even from one part of one's country to a strange part? You feel lost. Living in a city after being in a rural area, you find yourself lacking any of the familiar reference points to give you your bearings. People leave a place in which they are personally known to everyone, and they come to a place of tower-blocks where they are unknown. This means that they have to search afresh for religious or cultural or political forms of meeting. They have real difficulty in working out what their faith means in the city and relating that to the way they learned it back home. In light of all this, those of us who believe that the Christian faith is crucial for our lives today have been coming together in small groups. That allows us to set out to rediscover the meaning of faith in this new context.

Was there a gathering of such a group in his house each week?

> This is the way it is. We are in a Christian community of fifty to sixty people. We divide ourselves into small groups of eight or ten. It is in small groups that we can really get "deep" with one another, especially in matters of faith. The small size of the group is quite essential – there we find it possible to share our deepest feelings, the things which really disturb us. The meetings last for two to three hours and take place once every two weeks.

We also meet to celebrate our faith on a weekly basis. The form of the gathering for celebration and reflection is fairly well fixed. We start with reflection on some theological or pastoral theme that has preoccupied some of the groups. The theme will be made known beforehand to those who assemble and some material about it supplied. One group will be asked to do more work on it and to present it. What follows is a rich dialogue which clarifies understanding and action and which will continue in discussion in the smaller groups. We finish with a eucharist. The preparation of the eucharist will be delegated to selected people. It is a leisurely, spacious and festive gathering.

Bishop Labayan of the Quezon diocese in the Philippines admitted to a great gift on his appointment – his ignorance of how to be a bishop! So he called a pastoral congress, at the end of which he declared, in some such words as these: "I free you to find what the Word of God is saying to you today." At first nothing happened. Then nothing went on happening! People had been accustomed to being led "from above". After some time, they gravitated to one another, formed small communities, discovered fresh insights into the faith. Because Bishop Labayan showed patience, all this developed "from below".

A way of being church

It is characteristic of SCCs that they do not set up a substitute church but seek to give more adequate substance to what it means to be church in their particular time and circumstances. As Basque interviewees said, "they simply were the church trying to live its life faithfully". What SCCs insist on is space to make discoveries about what it is to "be church" and "live church", especially in situations where the local expression of church seems to be deficient in gospel content.

The determination to be no more than "a way of being church" is strong. The official church may produce separation by refusing acknowledgment and pushing SCCs away (as with Ovando y Bravo in Nicaragua). But SCCs want their discoveries to serve for the renewal of the whole church.

In its early years, the Iona community was in danger of being treated as a separate enterprise by the Church of Scotland. Strenuous and successful efforts were immediately made to remedy this. They illustrate the ecumenical value of appreciating the root from which one has sprung, and being open to all other Christian traditions. An Iona community board now reports to the annual general assembly of the Church of Scotland. Membership in the community is open to Christians of all traditions.

* * *

Here are two descriptions of SCCs at work, the first concentrating on the kind of people who may make up a small community, the other also on organization.

Ernesto Cardenal describes the small base community of people – fishermen, land workers, housewives, children – who met in Solentiname on Lake Nicaragua to discuss the Bible. He observes in the introduction to the biblical commentaries that grew out of this community:

> Not all those who do come take an equal part in the commentaries. There are some who speak more often. Marcelino is a mystic. Olivia is more theological. Rebeca, Marcelino's wife, always stresses love. Laureano refers everything to the revolution. Elvis always thinks of the perfect society of the future. Felipe, another young man, is very conscious of the proletarian struggle. Old Tomás Peña, his father, doesn't know how to read, but he talks with great wisdom. Alejandro, Olivia's son, is a young leader, and his commentaries are usually directed towards everyone, and especially towards other young people. Pancho is a conservative. Julio Mairena is a great defender of equality. His brother, Oscar, always talks about unity. The authors of this book are these people and all the others who talk frequently and say important things, and those who talk infrequently but also say something important, and with them William and Teresita and other companions who have taken part in the dialogues...
>
> I am wrong. The true author is the Spirit that has inspired these commentaries (the Solentiname *campesinos* know very well that it is the Spirit who makes them speak, and that it was

the Spirit who inspired the gospels). The Holy Spirit, who is the spirit of God instilled in the community, and whom Oscar would call the spirit of community unity, and Alejandro the spirit of service to others, and Elvis the spirit of the society of the future, and Felipe the spirit of proletarian struggle, and Julio the spirit of equality and the community of wealth, and Laureano the spirit of the revolution, and Rebeca the spirit of Love.*

***

Lunruma Omol from Kisumu, Kenya, described the SCCs' form of meeting in his area:

> We have an approach which is called the seven steps of Bible sharing – something used in a large part of Kenya. But we start with songs. Then we have a prayer just to welcome the Lord among us. Then all present share experiences and challenges which they have had to deal with since the last meeting, whether there is a one-week or two-week interval between. We have to discipline one another regarding time taken for this! Usually we restrict it to two minutes for each contribution. We read the word of God, then keep silence to reflect on it. Then we read the same passage again. Every member in turn can then share what has struck him or her about the reading, though not all will take the opportunity. Thereafter, those who wish to elaborate on that insight are free to do so. No one is inhibited. The next stage is when the members search for a way by which they could put the scripture reading into practice. This results sometimes in individual, sometimes in group actions. Examples could be visiting the sick or devoting the prayer of a whole week to some problem facing the community.

Would this cover social and political action?

> Yes. The decision might be to form a delegation to approach the mayor of the town. A couple of months ago members from several small Christian communities formed such a delegation to meet with the mayor on the shortage of water which was affecting the whole town. Members of the small Christian communities have formed a justice and peace group. They fight for the

---

* Maryknoll NY, Orbis, 1982.

rights of people who have been denied justice, confronting individuals and groups which are responsible for the injustice. Some of the members of the communities are lawyers and lend their weight to ensure, as far as possible, that justice is done. They also get alongside the poor and give them help, especially those who have no one else to whom to turn for basics such as food. In other cases, members will clean the houses of those who are unfit to do so themselves. I should have said that at each meeting there are reports on the actions decided on: how they were carried out, or what prevented them from being carried out. This helps other group members to be realistic about what can be done in expressing the word of God in their practical life.

Prayer will then include these experiences and the joys and sorrows which accompany them as people seek to live their faith today. They pray for one another. They seek God's blessing on the activities which they propose to undertake in God's name. The next step is to invite fresh concerns, which might have to do with the development of the group itself and which might also cover any financial matters to be sorted out. The meeting closes with the Lord's prayer and the last hymn. You will find that small communities in the shanty-towns have an unhurried meeting but those in urban areas are very time-conscious. At most, they would dedicate one and a half hours to each meeting.

Is the development of small Christian communities a strong one in your area?

In our archdiocese which partly covers the shanty-town areas, this development provides the best model for developing the life of the church. In the parish council, you would be unlikely to be elected if you did not have the experience of being in a small Christian community at the local level. That is considered to be a basic requirement in the lay apostolate. Environmental concerns, community development, combating alcoholism and many such things are integrated into the life of small Christian communities. They form a very strong feature of the mission of the church in our area.

Is the work done by small Christian communities fed into the official church, to the parish in each place?

"The movement is two-way."

How to get in touch?

SCCs do not advertise their presence. As, over a period, we began to be trusted, word got round and the trust spread. But there were still places where we knew SCCs existed but where no point of contact could be found. So:

a) I gathered what information I could at the offices of the World Council of Churches in Geneva. Since SCCs tended to keep a low profile, there was little to go on. But also, wherever possible, I got names and addresses of two people who knew the country in question – whether they were Christians was immaterial. On one occasion, I arrived in the Ivory Coast, consulted with a representative there, found the Geneva-gleaned information useless, phoned the two contacts, found both at home, went to see them and was told of two *centres d' animation*. Within hours of arrival, I was off to Bouaké in a kind of car-bus crammed with villagers.

b) I believed that to give attention to the poor you had to accept their conditions of living. So, starting with Asia, I sent a message ahead saying that I was not going to live in a hotel – could I be given a corner of the floor of a shack or shanty to curl up in at night, and could they spare me some of their food? To spend even a day or two sharing their conditions led to trust on their part, and they told me their stories as they never would have had I used a hotel. To ask for food rather than provide it, even in situations of great scarcity, meant that they were given the dignity of being the hosts and hostesses while I was their guest.

c) Our main recourse was prayer. It would go somewhat like this: "Look, Holy Spirit, if you want this visit to be fruitless for some reason that we cannot fathom, so be it. Otherwise, please put in our way people we need to meet."

Contemporary impact

Marcella Althaus Reid, Argentinian lecturer in New College, Edinburgh, Scotland, told me of the difficulty she had in getting students to pay serious attention to this phenomenon as one that is significant for the life and future of the whole church. The students thought of it as some equivalent to a star which came out of the unknown, blazed brightly for a while, and then disappeared into obscurity.

I told her she could share with them the following facts.

The third US national congress of SCCs was held in San Antonio, Texas, in August 2002, prepared on the basis of research funded by the Lilly Endowment and carried out by the Loyola Institute for Ministry. Thirty-seven thousand SCCs were identified. Since not all areas could be completely covered, it was hazarded that there might be up to fifty thousand in all. The research was limited to those in the Roman Catholic tradition in the USA.

During a visit to China in September 2001 concerned with establishing cultural exchange between British and Chinese churches, I took the opportunity to find out what I could about the development of house churches. I knew that, after the terror of the Cultural Revolution had abated, there had been phenomenal church growth, especially in the Protestant tradition. The principal of Wuhan theological college guessed there would be ten percent of the population in that tradition (she must have been thinking of those adhering to a religion of some kind). Then she added, "Half would be in registered churches and half in house churches."

I might also have mentioned to Marcella Reid my participation in a visit to Nicaragua the previous year in a team from Britain concerned with Jubilee 2000 and the Nicaragua solidarity campaign. In different parts of that country, we met small groups of people from base communities who could tell us of initiatives to improve the economic condition of the people, and of progress in dealing with violence against women in a macho culture. The members would introduce themselves and then name the SCC to which they belonged. These communities were the source of their vision and energy.

On the day that I wrote this, I received a letter from Bishop Thomas Dabre of the Vasai diocese, Maharashtra, India. In it, he testifies: "Recently we had a rally of 4000 people to animate SCCs. I realize that we can strengthen the church through small communities."

One, holy, catholic, apostolic church

The "marks of the church" were not brought into relationship with one another in the form in which we now know them until the 4th century, although the words identify characteristics of the church which have had significance from the start. Their association with one another has proved to be both natural and fruitful. They group some essential features, rather than providing an exhaustive check-list.

The formula is not explicit in the original text of the Nicene Creed. But when that creed is amplified in the creed of Jerusalem in 348, the words "one holy catholic church" are used; and the revision made by Cyril of Alexandria in 362 includes the words "... catholic and apostolic church". So it was in the 4th century that the words came together by magnetic attraction.

Small Christian communities have at times been called "para-churches" or "parallel churches" in an attempt to disown their full reality as part of the one, holy, catholic and apostolic church (although P.T. Forsyth – a well-known Scottish preacher in the late 19th/early 20th century – would have called them "outcrops of one rock").

Some time ago, I examined the marks of the church. If the actual life of SCCs should be tested in light of that examination, the reader may have means to judge whether he or she agrees with the hostile critics or with the verdict of the editor of the Australian magazine *OIKOS*, Bessie Pereira. In the summer 2002 edition she noted what she called "a marvellous conclusion" to such a comparison of the life of SCCs with the traditional marks of the church: "Small Christian communities do not stand 'outside' the church but move in the very flow of all that 'church' is."

2. The Marks of the Church: One

Unity is not a general word for "committed togetherness" in Christian theology. It is rather a word which points to a reality that underlies all life, makes sense of it and gives it direction and purpose. There is a basis for all hopeful relationships in human society and human history, its source lies beyond human life, affirms human life and acts in its favour. That source of unity on which the human race may draw to manage history creatively is the life of the Trinity.

In the life of God is the promise of fulfilment for all creation. For that life is lovingly directed towards the world and sacrificially poured out to effect the transformation in justice, truth and love of everything which has been brought into being. It follows that, to grow in oneness, the church must draw on this source and seek to be marked by its features. It must give weight to the large promise there represented for all humankind. It must make itself available to share in God's transforming purpose. It will seek the unity of humanity knowing that that requires of it concrete engagement in God's will being done on earth.

The oneness of the Trinity, it must be stressed, is a purposive oneness. A like oneness is not available to a church which cuts itself off from the struggle to bring new life to the world. It is in the struggle, and there only, that oneness may be found and wrought out. Especially since Jesus came proclaiming the kingdom (it was "kingdom" he announced, not "church"), it has been clear that whatever defaces, diminishes or destroys the quality and dignity of human life is hostile to God's promised unity. That same Jesus, in Colossians, is presented as at one and the same time head of the church and Lord of the world: and it is the kingdom of this world which is to become the ultimate kingdom (Rev. 11:15). Those who would have to do with God must accordingly be prepared to be drawn into a work of radical transformation of life as we find it. This entails belonging to an available and adaptable community, ready for whatever task is assigned – whether tasks are to the liking of the members or not, whether they themselves are put in the forefront of the battle or kept on the sidelines for as long as Jesus was. The church is to be just such a chosen instrument, available in the context of God's enterprise in favour of the whole household of humankind (the oikoumene). This enterprise defines the church's primary ecumenical task.

"Love me, love the work to which I have put my hand," says the Trinity to the church.

In his earthly life, Jesus prayed to the Father and sent the Spirit. Different parts are played by the Father, Son and Holy Spirit. But they are united in one mind and purpose. In the life of God, there is no conflict between oneness and difference. We can see an image of this in a loving family where parents and children may be as different as chalk and cheese, yet these very differences are made to enlarge and enrich life. There is a rejection of the life of the Trinity as a touchstone wherever on earth church authorities demand uniformity of belief and life. There is a similar rejection wherever small groups hive off and live in separation from the main body of believers. The body of Christ is called to illustrate on earth that reconciled diversity and mutual strengthening which derives from its trinitarian source.

Not domination and subordination, but mutual love

Oneness may have within it forms of subordination. But the subordination is never the kind imposed by the kings of the Gentiles on subjects (Matt. 20:25-28). First Corinthians 15:24-28 speaks of a subordination which may be called "functional", though I resist the word: it fails to convey the personal trust and understanding which allow an agreed operation to be undertaken, so I would rather speak of "assignment subordination" – a subordination designed to fulfil different parts of a total enterprise.

In that context, subordination is not thought of in terms of enlarged and diminished status. After all, the one who freely laid aside his glory and became a "nothing" *(doulos)* to undertake a task bears the name which is above every name in heaven and on earth and under the earth (Phil. 2:9-11). If, in the church on earth, the giving of authority to some and the subordinating of others is to reflect the nature of the Trinity, subordination must exist to effect purposes, never to exalt some and diminish others. Necessary signs of such relations will be that those who are given authority genuinely exercise it in a servant form and that those who are subordinate retain as much honour and voice as those to whom a larger authority is entrusted.

This trinitarian touchstone is a valuable one for assessing the extent to which existing church power structures have a gospel ring about them or contradict the gospel. Any assessment must be undertaken with great realism, since servant language has often been used as a cover-up for ways of life which are, in reality, full of domination! "We are servants of God," purr church authorities as they apply the screw.

In the Bible (see Gen. 4) a deep and committed earthly relationship which hints at the true relationship between God and humanity is that of husband and wife. In that relationship, two people are thought of as gaining "knowledge" of one another – getting deep into one another's being – not least through sexual intercourse.

In sexual intercourse, there is a penetrator and a penetrated. That may suggest domination and submission (and, in fact, may be so, and is so most blatantly in cases of rape). But where love rules, the reality can be that two people search one another out to the point where they pour their beings into one another. Submission becomes mutual. When New Testament writers struggle to define the true relationship of husband and wife (with, at the back of their minds, the particular problem faced by a Christian wife married to a pagan husband) they may advise conformity to whatever is current practice – though with a change of motivation. But they keep moving beyond that position to a recognition that those who are "joint heirs" to God's promises as husband and wife need to humble themselves before one another in mutual respect and love. How can subordination in the Godhead be expressed on earth other than in a relationship of mutual love? In the Corinthian text, Christ is mentioned in an "assignment completed" context. Then God, Father, Son and Holy Spirit will be all in all (1 Cor. 15:28). The Trinity is a circle.

That God the Lord is a community of love is to be expressed in an earthly sign – the existence of the whole body of believers offered for the life of the world. Nothing less than the whole body of believers is adequate to express on earth the reality of the Trinity as unity-in-diversity and to present to the world a sign, instrument and promise of humanity made one. While responsibility for parts of the work of spreading the gospel may be properly assigned to particular persons and can be forwarded through particular offices, these must never be looked on as if they formed some "concentrate" of unity or "depository" of gifts. There is a distortion of the body and a dishonouring of its different limbs and organs wherever one part is elevated as if it could stand for the whole. Who would say that the Son is more a source of unity in the Trinity than the Father or the Spirit? To fabricate "foci" of unity within the body on earth is simply to detract from the sign Jesus Christ left to be a promise for all humanity – the body itself.

The Trinity is a unity-in-truth. Expressed in earthly terms, such a unity will be one which does not gloss over the existence of awkward differences in traditions and cultural perceptions, in distinctive ways of thinking and doing, in varied political and religious stances. A church which roots itself in the life of the Trinity will not duck truth questions in order to preserve unity: Jesus Christ, source of its unity, is the Truth. Rather, it will provide evidence before the whole world that the unity which we have "in Christ" is deep and substantive enough to allow us to face one another openly and humbly regarding the things on which we are divided, to work them through so that all concerned are mutually instructed, to come to honest findings and follow them out however diverse our judgments, and in all this process to stay together.

Where people refuse to face up to the truth questions – in case they should offend one another and cause Christians to become divided – Christian community is absent. After all, what is distinctive about community "in Christ"? What, but that Christians' common rooting in Christ is strong enough for them to thrash out all kinds of differences and still remain in fellowship? Where such a sign of trinitarian faith exists, it means life for the world.

In taking the world seriously into account, the Trinity takes seriously where we ourselves are placed in history. It is in our particular place and time that obedience in community is to be offered. Jesus had his place and time. His conviction throughout most of his life was that he was sent only to the lost sheep of the house of Israel (Matt. 10:6, 15:24). It was the acceptance of that limitation which resulted in the end in his being lifted up and drawing all people to himself in a unity which was not limited by time, place or race. As the Trinity takes account of the terms of the world which it has brought into being, and respects these terms, the unity of those who share in the trinitarian initiative will, for the sake of larger possibilities, give careful attention to the terms offered in their specific places and times. There are opportunities, limitations and particularities to be respected by "all in each place". It is when these are taken into account that large breakthroughs become possible.

Although it is entirely appropriate that the church on earth should seek to understand and share the life of the Trinity, that life is not within the grasp of human beings. We understand it only fragmentarily. There will be forms and aspects of unity that will remain beyond us. They will wait in hiding to be discovered by others in different times and places.

Some aspects of unity will belong to that capping and crowning of life, the shalom of God which lies beyond history, in that state wherein we become fully part of the divine existence. Some will surprise us, as Jesus presents us with unexpected opportunities, accompanying his church in a kind of Emmaus walk in which he unfolds the past in the light of the future – his resurrected life being itself the main sign of incredible things God has in store for us. We must be expectant. He "is able to do exceeding abundantly above all that we ask or think". We must live in humility and awe. It is for God to say what is and is not to be entrusted to us in our time and place.

Does the emergence of SCCs threaten or enhance the church's unity?

Though SCCs have developed in a great variety of Christian traditions, reactions within the Roman Catholic Church may be particularly instructive because of its clear and strong authority structure.

Where the form of unity which already exists is taken as the touchstone, SCCs may be questioned, disowned or pushed away.

Such an assumption seemed to be made in the preparatory paper for the 2001 Catholic bishops synod, issued on 1 June of that year. SCCs are not specifically targeted, but reference is made to "ecclesiastical movements and new communities". While it is acknowledged that these "may be gifts of the Spirit", some are seen "on the periphery of dioceses and parish life and not beneficial to the local church". It is conformity to the existing standard of unity which is the touchstone here.

Outright rejection can also be found. During my visit to Nicaragua in 2000, the Masaya SCCs informed our group that they had a membership of around three hundred gathered in six main networks which also operated in smaller groups. Asked about the way in which the official church and Cardinal Ovando y Bravo looked upon that development, they replied, "The official church wants to have nothing to do with us. It pretends we do not exist."

The Managua communities elaborated,

The 1990s brought a change in attitude. We came up against pressures by the church hierarchy. They told us that good Christians don't get involved with politics. The values of the 1980s, solidarity, love, health, struggle, compassion and so on were turned on their head. Free education for all was lost. Free health care for all was lost. That leaves us with two objectives: on the one hand, we struggle to restore the values of the revolution, and on the other hand we struggle to prevent the Roman Catholic hierarchy from consolidating values which usurped these. In 1994, Cardinal Ovando y Bravo sent us a brief about the way we should live as good Catholics and appointed his

right-hand man to keep an eye on us. We offered to have a dialogue with him about this, but he refused, insisting that he was
the person in charge and had the right to lay down how we
should live and act.

No attempt was made to consider whether there might be
contributions from SCCs to a greater diversity which could
be reconciled within the ongoing life of the church, no
attempt at mutual submission or even dialogue but instead a
fiat from the official authority, no attempt at mutual learning,
no examination of the existing forms of coherence to discern
whether they were providing unity-in-the-truth. A power-
assumption militated against any attempt at relationship. The
contrast in approach with that of Bishop Labayan in the
Philippines, noted earlier, is striking.

* * *

When the communist power was broken in what was then
Czechoslovakia, the official church hierarchy tried to get
those who had not collaborated with the communists, as they
themselves substantially had done, to resume the old pattern.
The "dissidents" had formed SCCs in what they called "the
church of silence", in the underground, out of sight of the
secret police. They came under pressure to disband these.
Though they now felt free to contribute openly to the life of
the church in the parishes, the SCCs had proved to be a
source of life. They would not give them up. Bishop Fridolin
Zahradnik observed in an interview that, though persecution
must never be courted, God may give gifts which must not be
discarded when the situation changes. Reflecting on his six
years in jail he went on:

> We discovered that a bad situation also brought gifts. Opportu-
> nities for pastoral care appeared both inside and outside jails,
> such as had never been recognized previously. We tried to share
> these discoveries with traditional bishops. But they did not want
> to listen because they found security in the familiar way of
> doing things.
> My colleagues and I refuse to be tied to dioceses. We
> believe that we should concentrate on the poor, whom the tra-

ditionalists have neglected. We are not vestments-and-cathedral people but are dedicated to the service of human beings. On that basis, they find it difficult to cooperate with us. Add to that their bad consciences about collaborating with the communists and their rejections of the requirements of Vatican II, and you will appreciate their position! When I, myself, ordained priests or consecrated bishops, we were not in cathedrals but in workshops and basements. I think it made a more powerful impact on those present. For the development of the Emmaus enterprise with its concerns for those whom society cold-shoulders, I cover the whole of the republic.

It was during this interview that my interpreter stopped me and drew my attention to the fact that I started almost every question with "Bishop Fridolin..." That made it seem that he had a position of special status or honour. "He just has a job to do. We all have different jobs. Just call him by his first name as the rest of us do." Jan Klimes at that point showed true insight into the meaning of *episcopos*, an alternative word for "elder" or "presbyter" in the New Testament. The "epi" part is so often taken to have an "above" or "higher than" connotation. In fact, its connotation is one of directed energy. Those appointed to special positions have to give *concentrated attention* to the well-being of the church. No higher status is implied.

* * *

Almost as worrying as rejection is the uninstructed approval of some authorities who seem to think of the SCCs as the equivalent of an extra engine to add power to the ecclesiastical train while it goes along the same tracks as before. Bishop Kalilombe, extruded from Malawi during President Banda's time because he developed his diocese as a communion of SCCs (Banda felt he could keep his finger on the official churches, but a multitude of SCCs were proving too elusive), recorded his awareness of this aspect in an interview:

My feeling is that the leadership, hierarchy, bishops and so on, who today are officially encouraging and doing everything to build up these communities, have perhaps not realized all the consequences of the policy itself; and perhaps, if the policy were implemented and it started to have its logical consequences, they might get scared! I know that we have not fully reflected on all that it means to put the church in the hands of the laity. I know that the freeing of the laity, whom we cannot regulate in situations in which the hierarchy's grip on the church is not secure (you cannot control this from above), demands a real involvement in their day-to-day life, of which we bishops are not part. I think we have not yet seen how we will react if this development actually takes place. Therefore, we are still working with our own sort of illusion that we can build these communities and reap the benefits of this new developing church without having to break the normal structures of church life to which we cling. And so we are perhaps preparing for a day of judgment and a reckoning that hasn't been foreseen!

The life of the communities comes from a source to which they are called to be true – they are not just to be one, they are to be *one in Christ Jesus*. They are to be a sign of fulfilment of his prayer, "That they may all be one. As you, Father, are in me and I am in you, may they also be in us, so that the world may believe that you have sent me... I in them and you in me, that they may become completely one" (John 17:21,23).

"We are all in unity because we have all lived through an encounter with Jesus Christ which has turned our lives upside-down" is the testimony of the New Way. "It is Christ who summons the communities into existence and draws members together," reflected Ciro Castaldo in Naples. The Cité SCC in Brussels declared, in an open letter, "... the community is, by its art of living, the living remembrance of Jesus, a witness to him by its life..."

The following self-understanding, met by a contingent from Britain during a 1984 visit to SCCs in Italy, was agreed to be particularly striking: "The people of God must be self-convened before the living-Word-in-Christ, without human masters." The words "without human masters" served notice that any attempt to force the communities to conform to an ecclesiastical or secular ideology which could not stand up to the test of unity in Christ Jesus would be rejected. It was not that they presented themselves as an alternative church. They just needed and demanded enough space and a sufficient degree of autonomy to make discoveries about what it is to live the Christian faith today, not in order to break unity but to help the whole church to renew its life.

For a little while, I was the guest of a woman who lived in a poor quarter of San José, Costa Rica. She had little education, and her home, like all the houses around, was substandard and tiny for the eleven members of her family who lived there. Her husband left at five in the morning each day and worked until seven at night selling vegetables to support the family. They both belonged to a neighbourhood SCC which tried to see how changes that were needed in the area could be brought about. One morning, the woman was chatting with her friend. She said that the whole community must be roused to press for a fairer deal. Her friend protested that this was not her responsibility but that of the local government officials. Her tone sharpened:

> "Do you believe in Jesus Christ?"
> "Yes."
> "Do you think Jesus Christ came to change life so that it would become more the kind of life God wanted to see, or to leave it as it is?"
> "I suppose to change it. Yes, to change it."
> "Do you think Jesus Christ meant to change life by himself, or did he mean us to share the work with him?"
> (*Hesitantly*) "I know, he meant us to play a part."
> "Then how can you believe in Jesus Christ and let things stay as they are?"

* * *

A third type of response may be encountered. There are those, such as Bishop Labayan, who believe that the church "must make itself available to share in God's transforming purpose", who are open to a larger form of "reconciled diversity" that is already in evidence, who seek to honour and draw insights from those who struggle to live their faith at the grassroots of life and to engage in mutual accountability about their imaginative faithfulness in doing so. Such people treat Jesus Christ as the one, final authority and are prepared to go to meet him as he comes from the future with fresh gifts in his torn hands.

The experience of Paco is instructive. I lived with him in a *barrio* in Nicaragua. Previously, he had been my contact for the "Participation in Change" programme of the World Council of Churches, when he was based in Paraguay. He had seen the growth of basic Christian communities and acknowledged how disturbing this was for himself and his fellow priests in Nicaragua:

> We were scared, really scared. We saw these communities developing, encouraged them all we could, felt that they were of the Spirit. Then we discovered there was hardly anything committed to us as priests which they were not able to undertake in their ministry. We were teachers of the faith? Giving and receiving from one another around the scriptures, they were much more effective teachers of the faith. We were leaders of worship? Building into the liturgy their own music and drawing into it their own experience and suffering, they were much more skilled at worship-making than us. We at least had the mass? But it became clearer and clearer that we were not in control of the mass, that it was an act of the people together, whatever place of prominence we might take. And when it came to living out the faith in the world – of course they had a maturity and an awareness of what was at stake which went quite beyond anything that we were heir to.
>
> We were really scared! We thought that if we gave them their head, there would be no ministry left for us. We would be redundant. But we felt that it was commanded by the Spirit that the rich ministry of the people be allowed to develop. So we did not stand in the way. The result? What we lost is given back to us. The people understand the place of the ordained priesthood as never before. We have a ministry which is no longer over them, but with them. It was when we were prepared to give up the ministry as it was that God gave it back to us as a new thing.

Power needs to be given away if new ways of servant power are to be brought into play.

The unity which the church already experiences has been forged largely with one-sixth of the world's population which is articulate and educated. All over the world, imaginative efforts have been made to serve the other five-sixths. In our time, these have a new resource. The poor, the illiterate, the inarticulate have at last found in the SCCs a form of church which they genuinely can feel is their own. They meet in shanty-towns and gain fresh sense of their dignity in the eyes of God. The exodus from Egypt speaks to them of God's design to liberate all humanity from every oppression. The exodus Jesus accomplished at Jerusalem assures them of a prevailing power beyond all earthly oppressive powers. The Holy Spirit endows them with gifts and strength to seek the kingdom of God and God's righteousness right where they are.

* * *

I took the following notes from an SCC gathering in San Miguelito, Panama:

> One night, when a planned engagement fell through, I wandered among the homes of the community. There I met a man with whom I had previously talked while he was washing down a car. Nine months before, Bill had been a hopeless drunk. Now, converted, he lived by doing odd jobs. I asked if there was anything happening in the area which would be interesting for me to visit. He said he was now a lay pastor and was just about to conduct a liturgy of the word, and that I was very welcome to come along.
>
> The bare house in which the people gathered was really one small room with two partitions breaking it up. For a good part of the service, two of the children of the household were crying intermittently. Occasionally, one would get up to pull back the curtain of one of the partitions and gaze at us. Outside, the dogs barked and howled, competing with a transistor radio. On the kitchen table was a cross with a lighted candle on either side. Over his open-necked shirt, Bill placed a stole and was ready to start. About ten neighbours, most in their early twenties or thirties, pressed in, some bringing their own chairs or stools with them. I shared a tatty couch with an older man.

There was an introductory section in which people sang and gave responses. Then a passage from the Acts of the Apostles, used throughout the parish that week, was taken for study. Practically everyone participated in building up an understanding of the passage. At one point, Bill was pushing them too strongly in emphasizing God's presence in the midst of life. They would not have this. "We know God is in the thick of things where we are," they said. "We believe that. But that is not all. God is also beyond us. We do not know how God can be with us and beyond us. But that's just the way it is." After about forty minutes of Bible study, those who took part were asked to offer prayers, and all but two responded. Another song was sung, there were one or two more responses and the service ended.

* * *

In Tarlac, La Paz, in the Philippines, I met with a Christian community of small farmers who had been brought to the edge of starvation. In successive years their rice crops had been destroyed by a plague of rats or by disease or by typhoon and flood. "Some days", said a woman, "we had only one cup of rice for my children, my husband and myself. But, by the grace of God, we did survive." They did more than survive. Together they deepened their life of faith. Our meeting started with an act of worship. When it came to prayer, about fourteen people took part, and about the same number contributed when there was a reflection on a passage of scripture. There were people in their community who were worse off than themselves, landless. Now that there had been a good harvest from their small rice paddy fields, the landless were given freedom to use these fields to plant mongo (beans), and those who were disabled or old got a portion of the harvests. Living, worshipping, sharing possessions were all of a piece with them.

* * *

The following testimony came from Guatemala.

I know of an Indian community of very, very poor people. They live in cardboard shacks under a bridge on the outskirts of

Guatemala City. A small group of eight people, they get together, once again with the Bible as a basis. They read the Bible and they try to apply what they read to their lives.

It's a very small community, one that should be growing, and hopefully, it will grow. Their group discussions usually lead them to take some kind of action to help all the folk who live under the bridge – about fifty or sixty families. One of their recent actions was to go to the town hall in Guatemala City, and demand clean water for all these people. They live there without any water except when it rains. They would see that initiative as an action flowing from their Christian commitment, from Jesus' commitment to the poor. They say that if they aren't working for these others, what's the point of working at all.

Through the life of SCCs, the church can have a larger unity in which the poor are not only acknowledged but given voice and place. But is there a new divisiveness based on the idea that only the poor can be "real church"?

In 1980, I visited SCCs in Mexico, Guatemala, El Salvador, Nicaragua, Panama and Venezuela. In two of these countries, I was met with the same question. "We hear there are also SCCs in Europe. How can that be in affluent Europe?" By the time the question was asked, I had been able to learn much about the development of SCCs in the countries concerned. So, instead of answering in the abstract, I told stories of European SCCs which resonated with their own. They were astonished. "But these are our kin," they said. "They are not oppressed by poverty the way we are. Their young people are not hounded by death squads. They don't have Molotov cocktails thrown against a door or through a window. But, allowing for a difference in circumstances, they seek God's kingdom as we do in small communities. How can this be? The broad Atlantic lies between. They did not spark off us or we them!" In no time, they agreed that what we were experiencing was spontaneous combustion of the Holy Spirit all over the world. It is this manifestation of the Spirit that provides unity in the great variety of countries in which SCCs have developed.

3. The Marks of the Church: Holy

The word "holy", in the first instance, may be applied to God alone. But since we are called to live God's way and are given the Holy Spirit to strengthen us in doing so, it applies also in a derivative way to human beings. As early as the 7th century BC, the law of holiness, in Leviticus 19:2, depicts Moses being commanded to say to the people of Israel: "You shall be holy, for I the Lord your God am holy."

When human beings seek to relate in some such way to God (or, in other religions, to gods) they may be overwhelmed by the distance between their earthly life and the divine life (as was Job when God said, "Where were you when I laid the foundations of the earth?"). For them, the calling to be holy conveys the need to stand in awe before the mystery of such greatness and power. That has its place. But the core of the nature of holiness lies deeper.

The original Hebrew and Aramaic words for "holy" and the main such Greek word in the New Testament all have the same essential connotation, that of "separating off". The calling to be holy is a calling to live a separated existence. This has sometimes been taken to imply being separated from the world and all its affairs. In the Old Testament, the prophets, proclaiming a God of justice, called people to cut themselves off from ways of oppression of the poor and vulnerable and to "let justice roll down like waters, and righteousness like an ever-flowing stream" (Amos 5:24). They were asked to break away from a way of life which God could not countenance and fight to change their situation so that it mirrored God's justice. The separation is not from the world but *in* the world *for* God's way of life.

When members of a praying church in Antioch were told by the Holy Spirit to separate Barnabas and Saul for a particular work, the word used is one for "setting boundaries" (Acts 13:1-3). The boundaries are not those which would cut off the two apostles from ordinary life and its hazards nor from ordinary people and their ways. What they are separated from are all kinds of distracting options, in order to fulfil God's particular mandate. This is made clear in Acts 16:6-10. Unevangelized countries were debarred to Paul, a missionary to his fingertips, not so as to thwart his zeal but to direct it, that the invitation from Macedonia might be heard and answered.

Jesus himself said, "I have a baptism with which to be baptized; and what stress I am under until it is completed!" (Luke 12:50). When he set his face to go to Jerusalem, there were safer roads he might have taken. In Gethsemane, he prayed that he might not have to drink the cup of suffering and shame, but ended, "nevertheless, not my will but yours be done". Jesus is called the "holy and righteous one" (Acts 3:14) because he accepted his baptism of fire, separated himself from all other options in order to ensure that humanity might have life abundant.

* * *

A poor woman opened the eyes of a nun to a true under-standing of holiness.

In Brussels, we met a Solima nun who worked in Pueblo Jovén, Brazil. She told us:

> There are very poor people there. There is no water, there is no light, it is terrible. The bishop did not want to renew the con-tract with us.
>
> One of the things he said was: "You are no longer involved in the things that are holy." I told this to one of the women of Pueblo Jovén. She was very angry. She said, "For the bishop what is holy is all that is happening inside his church. For me what is holy is the future of my people."
>
> The Saturday before Easter I came back to my convent. It's a big convent. They had the celebration of Easter with water, light, etc. There is a priest in the convent who is a very artistic man. In the chapel there was a beautiful scene, beautiful vest-ments, water, a very beautiful lighted candle and beautiful music. I came from Pueblo Jovén where there was no water or light. I left the chapel and afterwards I said, "*This* is the de-generation of the liturgy."

Cleanliness – a substitute for holiness

God's demand that his people live a holy life keeps get-ting reduced at different points of history to a requirement that they keep pure and remain clean. Assonance contributes to the confusion (though to say so is not to ignore the sin which seeks security in impeccable observance of routines – a saying from the north-east of Scotland observes "cleanliness is next to Godliness, and it's a damn sight easier"). The word *hagios* resonates to the old Greek word *hagos* which refers to an object of awe; and to it the word *hages*, the word for clean, resonates in turn.

Once forms of uncleanness were specified and graded according to their seriousness, once certain procedures for purification were prescribed, the priestly class had a weapon for control and exploitation in its hands. In spite of the doctrine that God had given women and men equal dignity and had entrusted to them together the charge of the earth, women were made the chief victims of purification requirements. Their bodily functions condemned them to regular periods of "uncleanness". When a girl was born, the time of ritual defilement was twice as long as it was for a boy.

In spite of the doctrine that all human beings are made in the image of God (Gen. 1:26,27), the handicapped were treated as being constitutionally unclean and were debarred from the priesthood.

In spite of God's bias towards the poor, the prescription that animals for sacrifice should be without spot or blemish ensured that priests lived on the fat of the land and the poor had to struggle to afford sacrificial offerings.

Came the prophets, and the very idea of cleansing was quite transformed. What was it that soiled people's hands? Not the dirt of ritual impurity. Something much more defiling. The blood of their fellow human beings. The demand for cleansing, in this context, became a demand for the establishment of justice. There was a complete reversal of the emphasis previously made. To be clean and pure in God's sight was now to accept whatever dirt stuck to you as you engaged with others in the struggle to establish God's way of life in face of many, many forms of oppression. Isaiah 1:16 expresses the turnaround:

There is blood on your hands
wash yourselves and be clean
cease to do evil
learn to do right, pursue justice and champion the oppressed.

Purity of life has to do not with bodies (total lives) which are stainless, but with bodies which are offered as a living sacrifice in union with Christ's. The alternative to blood on one's hands is resisting to the point of shedding your blood, that God's kingdom may come and God's will be done on earth.

Baptism is entry into sacrificial engagement. It is an abandonment of the search for purity achieved through conformity, clean-handedness, an irreproachable reputation. As is said in Romans 6:3, "Do you not know that all of us who have been baptized into Christ Jesus were baptized into his death?" – the death of the one who made himself of no reputation and gave up life for our redemption. Baptism requires us to throw our lives on the scales for a new world. The world from which we are then to keep ourselves unspotted is life organized in opposition to God's kingdom.

Since, for the Hebrews, the heart was not the seat of intuitive and emotional responses but the seat of thought and will and purpose, to be "pure in heart" is to have life directed, single-mindedly, to doing God's will in the world, whatever dirt may stick in consequence.

"There is always an energy in the holy which is lacking in the pure and clean."* The concept of "the holy" has in it the dynamic of movement to the new creation of God's promise. Holiness of life has to do with being in that movement, taking the risks involved. The new heavens and earth are the home of justice (2 Pet. 3:13) and life is entrusted to human beings so that they may realize on earth some part of the fullness of the justice which awaits (examine here 1 Cor. 1:9; Col. 1:22; 1 Thess. 3:13, 5:23; 2 Pet. 3:14).

---

* O. Procksch, in Gerhard Kittel, *Theological Dictionary of the New Testament*, Grand Rapids MI, Eerdmans, 1964, vol. 1, p.89.

In the pursuit of holiness, the world comes into its own as the appropriate vehicle for representing and expressing God's loving initiatives (as in the incarnation – "God so loved the world..."). Those who take the way of holiness will be up to their elbows in conflicts and compromises, in strenuous engagement for whatever forms of justice can be realized at a particular time (this dynamic also resides in the Greek word *dikaiosune*, righteousness) – for it is the demands and pressures of this world that provide the only appropriate milieu for growth in the holy life.

Those who are called to be holy as God is holy (1 Pet. 1:15) are to be "children of obedience", available and on their toes for whatever God wants them for as God seeks to bring the new order into being in the midst of the old. Those who remain determined to keep their noses clean may well refuse a holy calling.

The Holy One is a dynamic presence in the world. As people became aware of this, the pagan and early pagan-influenced Hebrew interpretations of God's otherness came to be drastically changed. God's holiness, it dawned on people of faith, does not lie in some otherness which is designed to humble and crush us, a *mysterium tremendum et fascinans* which both attracts and menaces. The otherness of God, which makes a glaring contrast between the one God and other gods, and between God and us, lies in what God, the all-powerful, has chosen to be separated *from* and *for*. God deliberately refuses the path human beings might expect a god to take. The Almighty takes a strange way for anyone to whom divinity is ascribed. The one who has all power in heaven and on earth has chosen to be set apart *from* ways of exercising Godhead which would, if we refused compliance, over-ride our wills (and, make no mistake, God holds all the trump cards), and has chosen to be apart *for* a way of exercising Godhead which makes God weak and vulnerable. The Lord of all will depend on human beings becoming willing partners in God's purpose.

The decision on God's part not to bypass us but to win us for partnership, is expressed in the conclusion of the story of

Noah and the flood. God will not bring human beings to heel by the threat of destruction, nor will he go back to the drawing board and produce an unfailingly obedient humanity. Indeed, destruction which we draw upon ourselves may be a sign of God's respect for us. In response to "here am I, send me", a message may be entrusted which calls people to the way of life. This may meet with ears stopped and eyes closed. Then "cities waste and without inhabitant", i.e. clear evidence of the consequences of rejecting God's way, alone may be what will give human beings a fresh chance willingly to turn in a new direction (see Isa. 6).

God chooses to be "the Holy One in the midst". It goes against all human instincts that God should be seen to take such a risk. "Up there" God could be safe, clean, out of it, commanding impressively. But God "in the midst", not forcing human beings to conform, chooses to become incredibly exposed and vulnerable. It is shocking that the one whom we know as Father makes himself "of no reputation", lays aside his glory (a word which has in it a sense of back-up from a "weight of armies"), remains invisible lest God crowd us or compel us. The way God the Father chooses to exercise Godhead is marked by the frailty of love. That is what finds expression in the visible and incarnate life of the Son.

What caused demons to see in someone who is as "human as they make them" the Holy One of God (Mark 1:24)? What caused Peter to go scrabbling on his knees among the fishing nets (Luke 5:8) and to refuse to get his feet washed (John 13:8)? An awareness and an awe were present much more profoundly than could be invoked by the pagan sense of taboo or the Hebrew unwillingness to name the Name. There was a realization that in a human being as defenceless as any other born of woman, we come in raw and direct contact with the reality of God Most High! What overwhelms us as no application of bare power can, what overwhelms us and still leaves us our personal freedom? God naked, appealing to us, bent on realizing in partnership with us a new order of life.

If challenged, God produces no further evidence to convince us that one who chose to be revealed in such weakness is indeed God the Lord. There is nothing to back up the claim but the consistent, persistent, non-retractable investment of the power of Godhead in the salvation of the world. As Amos says (4:2), God will swear by God's own holiness. It is all God has left when instruments of compulsion are laid aside. God has chosen to be set apart from other ways for this way. The fact declares God's holiness. We are called to see and believe.

A royal priesthood, a holy nation

Holiness is not just one characteristic among others of God's nature and of the life to which we are called. It is the energy on which life flourishes, the root from which life is renewed. When are God's people seen to meet the claim made on them, "You shall be holy, for I am holy"? When they are a spring of new life in the world. The holiness code of Leviticus 19 is quite specific. Being holy as God is holy means, for instance, leaving gleanings in fields and trees to be food for the poor, not cheating or oppressing others by holding back the day's wages of a day labourer, respecting the deaf and the blind, seeing justice done to poor and great alike.

The church is a "holy nation" (1 Pet. 2:9). That does not mean it should consist of spiritual athletes, or of people who live twelve feet off the ground, nor yet be characterized by those officially elevated to sainthood by the church (which likes to exercise proprietorial control over the values and virtues it thinks appropriate to sainthood). The "holy nation", the "people of God's own possession", comprises the rag-tag-and-bobtail army which, with its faults patent for every-one to see, engages the enemy in God's name. The saints of God, the holy ones, are a morally and spiritually motley crew. It is not merit and attainment which qualify them. It is not unusual competence. It is simply that they are chosen and sent just as they are. It is their readiness to be chosen and sent which makes them holy people.

All these – unlikely people, many of them, to be enlisted at all – are in for a surprise when they persist in the Way.

Sanctification is the gift God has up a sleeve for the kingdom's sake. They find that, when they surrender life to God and offer their lives to be a living sacrifice, they blossom and flower *as themselves*. They should have known from Jesus, of course, that it is those who lose life who find it, and from John the Divine that there awaits them a new name, written on a white stone, which sums up all that they have it in themselves to be (Rev. 2:17).

What will it mean, concretely, for the church to live a holy life?

It will need to "walk on two legs" as it has been put in Europe, or to "read two letters" as it has been expressed in Central America – to read the mind of God/to read situations/and to relate the two dynamically. It is thus that action can be taken to transform life in the direction of the kingdom, God's way for living penetrating all our relationships and institutions. The Bible must be given close, prayerful attention with its revelation concerning how God works in history, especially in the incarnation of Jesus Christ. Situations faced have to be given close scrutiny, researched and analyzed thoroughly, so that we know what we have to cope with and how the resources of the gospel may be brought to bear.

SCCs are a sign of promise for the church. For them the scriptures are a new book, very relevant to their lives, which they search diligently. To take stock of issues they believe they are called to deal with, they often use the see-judge-act approach: see – look closely at what actually has to be faced, getting beyond superficial impressions; judge – weigh up what is there and the options open for dealing with it; act – to make a change to establish signs of God's kingdom. This is part of an ongoing process.

Lunruma Omol from Kisumu, Kenya, has already indicated this:

> In the SCCs, at each meeting there are reports on the actions decided on: how they were carried out, or what prevented them from being carried out. This helps other group members to be realistic about what can be done in expressing the word of God in their practical life. Prayer will then gather into it these ex-

periences and the joys and sorrows which accompany them as people seek to live their faith today. They pray for one another. They seek God's blessing on the activities which they propose to undertake in God's name.

* * *

When I interviewed members of SCCs, I always had a question about the part the Bible played in their lives. In every case it was a source of life. Here are a series of short responses from SCCs in Western Europe, and one or two illustrations from other parts of the world, rounding off with commitments of the Iona community.

Andalusia: The Bible "is the central permanent point of reference for all the thinking and the action of the groups. It takes a crucial place in helping Andalusian people to do battle for the future of this region. The Bible is read before the celebrations we have, and then studied afterwards. The biblical witness is related to Andalusian self-government and people's concrete problems – especially the exploitation of labour and the need for the redistribution of land (title to enough to support a family), unemployment due to industrialized farming, and immigration to other parts of Spain and to other countries. Many cooperate with one of the most powerful trade unions, the rural workers trade union, and occupy land when people lack it and are suffering hunger."

Enderestrasse community, Vienna: "The Bible is the basis of our Christian life... BCCs in Brazil have taught me that it isn't necessary to study very much to understand the Bible. It's more important to pray, to meditate on the Bible and to act accordingly; to involve yourself in social life and society and to fight (though not with force, not with violence) for more justice in this world. I don't think we do this enough here in Austria. That is something we need to learn."

Oporto: The Bible as a source of illumination: "When it is read without defensiveness and is allowed to make its authentic impact, it penetrates to the marrow in its challenge to us to live life like Jesus – really and truly like his."

San Marco, Rome: "Until Vatican II, Bible reading was forbidden to individuals and groups among the laity. Every second week, the BCC gathers around the Bible and seeks interaction between it and everyday life."

Nijmegen, The Netherlands: "The group had started with a form of life which had been ecclesiastical and fairly traditional. But there was a study and reflection on the Bible and the Bible itself produced a deliverance from the heavy weight of the tradition of the church because that tradition pushed the group back to the original sources of the church, beyond the particular historical types of development. So it became possible for the members of the group to stand attentive and open to the message in the Bible without being caged by the traditions through which the interpretation of the Bible had passed in history."

Turin: "A different approach to the Bible, to the New Testament, was needed, open to the people. It needed to be made the basis of living. It needed to be interpreted from working-class perspectives. People began to see the New Testament as a message of liberation not only for the working class but for all mankind through struggle. [Till now the Bible has been regarded]... as a mysterious book to be kept in the hands of priests."

Oporto: "The true place of prayer is where the actual situation people have to face and wrestle with meets the Bible." Question: "How would you describe the community at the time of the revolution?" Answer: "I would say simply that they were 'people journeying with the Bible', seeking to discover how the Bible is to be situated today, for instance in relation to our present political context."

Basque: [The Bible] "has a central place... and allows us to have a new kind of theology."

Clichy-sous-Bois: "To confront the gospel in the Bible, day after day, has brought a great freshness into life."

Dutch statement: "The community has reappropriated the Bible of which it is the exegete, adopting the angle of vision given by God who takes sides, determined to liberate."

Utrecht: "The Bible was a bit on the back shelf in the early 1970s, but there has now been a change. The BCCs in Holland have no reason for existence and no future unless they let the Bible stories function effectively within the situations people face today."

Gospel, Neuchatel: "The Bible is always present in spirit or reality, and most of the time we try to illuminate a problem starting with or going to a biblical text... We always seek to link this with the present time and to the problems of our world, for the text has social, economic, cultural and political implications."

Padeao da Legua, Oporto: "To root daily life more effectively in the word, we have divided into four according to the places where members live, so that they can address themselves to particular local situations as well as to larger issues. [The Bible shows] the feeblest, the least have their part to play in God's action to liberate humanity. We find that astonishing and exciting."

Emmaus, near Turin: "Ours is a communal reading in which we try to be alert and alive to what the word of God is saying to the concrete circumstances of our daily life. This is in contrast with the abstract and 'spiritual' interpretation of the Bible in local churches. The openness to the Bible is one of the two points of concentration of our BCC in its recent life."

Biel/Bienne, Switzerland: "... the struggle is to live life in terms of an encounter with the Bible. Here what is important is to live in solidarity with people in one's own area, in one's own region, in one's own country and in the world as a whole... Everyone is committed within a sector of society..."

* * *

It was the Bible that made the impact on the small fishing village of Bagakay in the Philippines, causing them to form a village SCC. What produced the change? Until the early 1970s, they had thought of the church as being for rich people in towns, not for the likes of them. Then one of the younger members of the community was given the chance of education. At school, he encountered the Bible. The villagers would gather round when he returned and he would read and explain it. They found that Jesus' world was their world! In it, they met oppressive landlords, questions of tenants' rights and responsibilities, the tough business of finding and catching fish, uncertain harvests, the lighting and cleaning of houses, the baking of bread. They found hope as they listened. Then they began to use their own minds, and drew more on their own experience, challenging the interpretations of their instructor. They discovered the dignity God gave them as people made in God's likeness.

They became awkward people, no longer prepared to fit in tamely with the schemes of the powerful. The authorities labelled the challenge to their power "communist", although the people did not know what communism was. It was the gospel which had given them fresh life and hope. Pressures on them mounted. An old lady summed up their situation to the nods of all around: "To tell the truth, we are afraid. But God's word is more powerful than our fears. We will all have to die some day. We have decided we may as well die for a worthwhile cause."

Three Italian SCCs described to me the quite different routes they had taken to reappropriate the scriptures – with this in common: rejecting interpretations of the priest as the sole authority, they moved through the use of commentaries to find some way to draw on the wisdom and expertise of scholars.

Speaking of the research into SCCs in the USA carried through by the Loyola Institute for Ministry, Bernard J. Lee observed, "Their probing of scripture (usually lectionary based) and their own experiences is the centre-piece of SCC activity." At another point, he noted that there was a weakness in political and social engagements which should have been an outflow of the scriptural perceptions (after all, they had no such hindrance as had the Czechs and Hungarians under the communists – where such activity would have invited a harsh crackdown from the secret police).

A Baptist pastor in Rome, whose people had made common cause with Roman Catholic SCCs, spoke to me of how necessary it was to keep a dynamic relationship between God's self-revelation and the human situation. He spoke thus of his own experience: "Some groups, unwilling or unable to cope with the tension between new movement and traditional institution, had been reassimilated by the institution. Others had invested totally in political activism. They faded away, unable to be bearers of the new life." He concluded tellingly, "We must never retreat into the Bible or into politics."

The discovery of the way of holiness was particularly striking in the experience of SCCs in the Netherlands early in their life. Representatives came together in an attempt to define priorities. What about the Bible? "The priest's book", they concluded, "interpreted to fit in with his narrow way of looking at life. Out of the window with it!" "What about the mass?" "A rigmarole which ministers to the priest's control over the people. Out of the window with it!" What, then, is the real heart of the gospel? "Justice-making," they decided. "We will concentrate on fighting for and establishing justice."

After several months they came together again. To one another they confessed: "We don't know what justice is without the Bible! We are not nourished for the struggles to establish justice without the sacrament!" And how much richer was their fresh appreciation of the word and sacrament because they had had the courage to depart from what did not seem real, and the insight to keep an eye on what they had discarded in case there was more in it than they had appreciated!

The small communities in Hungary and Czechoslovakia testified to the central significance of prayer during their years of underground existence. There was even a Czech testimony that, if all overt means were denied, prayer directly produced political change.

It was in the Ipil diocese of Mindanao in the Philippines in 1982 that I came across one of the most constructive relationships established between professional theologians and those who were "living the faith at ground level". In the diocese, there were 1200 BCCs. Each week they gathered round the Bible, looking for light to help them deal with the oppression from which they suffered under the Marcos dictatorship, plagued as they were on the one hand by poverty and on the other by threats of armed gangs. Work on the Bible was prepared for two or three months ahead.

The start was with peasants and workers. They would identify concrete issues in situations they faced which needed to be addressed. With their growing knowledge of the Bible, they would identify texts which might help them to deal with these issues from a faith perspective. Only then could the professionals come in. Almost inevitably, they would be greatly enlightened when they heard the texts of the Bible which the people considered to be relevant. They might then go on to say: "You suggest consulting this part of the Bible. But are you aware that that other part seems to speak in flat contradiction of it?" "Then we must study both," would come the reply. Thereafter, they worked together. It becomes a matter not of specialists building up the church, but of the whole church building itself up in love (Eph. 4:16), by preparing biblical resources for nourishing and directing lives.

* * *

In the rule of the Iona community, of which I have been a member for 62 years, attention to the will of God is to be immediately related to action in the world for justice and peace. The following comes from the rule as it appears in the 2003 members booklet:

The rule of the Iona community

Our fivefold rule calls us to:
1) daily prayer and Bible-reading;
2) sharing and accounting for the use of our money;
3) planning and accounting for the use of our time;
4) action for justice and peace in society;
5) meeting with and accounting to each other.

Daily prayer and Bible reading
We are asked to pray for each other, for our common concerns, and for the wider work of the church, on a daily basis. We are

also asked to read the Bible on a regular and frequent basis. Together with prayer requests and topics in the members booklet, the use is commanded of *Pray Now*,* *With All God's People*,** or such other resources as mentioned in the community's "spirituality tool-kit".

Justice and peace commitment
We believe:

1) that the gospel commands us to seek peace founded on justice and that costly reconciliation is at the heart of the gospel;
2) that work for justice, peace and an equitable society is a matter of extreme urgency;
3) that God has given us partnership as stewards of creation and that we have a responsibility to live in a right relationship with the whole of God's creation;
4) that, handled with integrity, creation can provide for the needs of all, but not for the greed which leads to injustice and inequality and endangers life on earth;
5) that everyone should have the quality and dignity of a full life that requires adequate physical, social and political opportunity, without the oppression of poverty, injustice and fear;
6) that social and political action leading to justice for all people and encouraged by prayer and discussion is a vital work of the church at all levels;
7) that the use or threatened use of nuclear and other weapons of mass destruction is theologically and morally indefensible and that opposition to their existence is an imperative of the Christian faith.

As members and family groups we will...

8) engage in forms of political witness and action, prayerfully and thoughtfully, to promote just and peaceful social, political and economic structures;
9) work for a British policy of renunciation of all weapons of mass destruction and for the encouragement of other nations, individually or collectively, to do the same;

---

* Edinburgh, St Andrew Press, 2002.
** Geneva, WCC, 1990.

10) work for the establishment of the United Nations Organization as the principal organ of international reconciliation
and security, in place of military alliances;
11) support and promote research and education into non-
violent ways of achieving justice, peace and a sustainable
global society;
12) work for reconciliation within and among nations by international sharing and exchange of experience and people,
with particular concern for politically and economically
oppressed nations.

4. The Marks of the Church: Catholic

The word "catholic" is not a biblical word. But it was adopted from early times to express a major perception about the nature of the church's life. In the development of the church since then, it has been used to attempt to validate exclusive claims for particular forms of the church. Such claims contradict the word's inherent meaning. "Catholic" is an ample word, a word about what Christian communities are to keep growing into. It is a "we're-not-there-yet-we-press-on" word. It holds in it nuances suggesting colourfulness, diversity, comprehensiveness, roundedness.

What becomes of it when it is conjoined to a particular word such as "Roman"? The conjunction of the two could imply that the church identifies itself as a sect (i.e., a part of the *una sancta* acting as if it were all that mattered). Alternatively, it could point to two aspects of the church's own reality: both that historical root from which the church has grown, which provides one main source of its identity, "Roman", and the larger dimensions of life it needs to be continually expanding into, which provides the other word, "catholic". Similarly, the idea of an Anglican world communion is a contradiction in terms – unless what is decisive is what that communion is growing into rather that what it has grown from (which is also due proper recognition). "The Church of Scotland" is a nonsensical description if it is understood as a denominational claim to exclusive status. But the name could also be interpreted to register a hope that some all-embracing form of church will be attained which will at last make sense of the title.

As far as present knowledge goes, the first association of the word "catholic" with the word "church" occurred around 112 A.D. in Ignatius' letter to the church in Smyrna (8.2). There, it was used both to denote the whole body of believers vis-a-vis particular congregations, and to distinguish the church from sects.

The four features identified by Cyril of Alexandria in his *Catecheses* (348 A.D.) form an interpretation of "catholicity". His pointers very obviously do not form a description of the church "as is" but suggest characteristic features which the church must hope will mark its life more and more as it moves through history. He spoke of:

a) The church's extension in space

Since his time, the church has penetrated to regions of the world then unknown. In the ecumenical movement, one gain derived from awareness of a larger church has been a rediscovery of gifts given to non-Western parts of the church from the earliest centuries; e.g., Eastern liturgies which do not stress God's almightiness so much as God's merciful and loving nature (in the New Testament the word "almighty" occurs only once, and that in quotation: 2 Cor. 6:18). Other faiths and ideologies have now been affirmed – on the bases that (1) Christ everywhere puts pressure on human beings, including those who do not acknowledge him, to establish righteousness; (2) human beings respond differently in different cultural contexts; and (3) these responses must be respected as well as critically evaluated. The idea of extension in space has itself been extended and now includes spheres of human activity as well as areas of geographical church location. The phrase of the WCC's New Delhi assembly in 1961, "all in each place", affirms this wider understanding.

b) The church's completeness of doctrine

Cyril of Alexandria no doubt intended to suggest that Christian doctrine was complete in his time. We, through the centuries, discover that we no sooner reach one hilltop in clarifying the faith than others appear ahead and challenge us to fresh effort. In any case, doctrine can claim to be rounded and well-founded only when it is the product of the *consensus fidelium* – God's whole people reflecting on their lived faith and coming to a mind about its essentials (this is the decisive *magisterium* or teaching authority). Through living the faith in relation to their time, the generations develop fresh resources for understanding it.

Doctrine is taking shape, in our day, in fiery furnace experiences, in dance, in song, in testimonies before tribunals, in poetry, in painting, etc., as well as in word formulation.

When George Candlish managed the Church of Scotland theatre, the "Gateway", in Edinburgh, he suggested that the only adequate exegetical vehicle for the Book of Revelation was ballet. Only at the end of history, when people see God face to face and develop praise with every instrument and in every mode of expression, will doctrine be complete. Systematic theology is not a construct of abstract propositions but a shimmer of changing light.

c) The church's adaptation to the needs of every person

Cyril could hardly have foreseen how this perception would, in the course of history, open doors to people of different races, classes and sexes, to children as well as to older people, to the acceptance of different word-languages, image-languages, concept-languages. The findings of the council of Nicea are important in this respect. There it was affirmed that in the incarnation the Word had become not *andros* but *anthropos*, not "man" but "humankind". On this interpretation, the alienation between human beings referred to in Genesis 3 has been dealt with; in Christ, new partnership can now be established between women, children and men beyond all class, race, age or sex limitations (Gal. 3:28).

d) The church's perfection of spiritual grace and power

What would Cyril have written had he foreseen the crusades: had he envisaged the tapestry in Seville of the Virgin throwing her cloak protectively around Columbus and the other *conquistadores* as they set out with a cross and sword on their civilizing mission in the New World; had he anticipated religious wars; had he measured the impact wherever the church has been accorded ceremonial acknowledgment and place in return for silence in face of the secular arm's bloody work? Of all the features of catholicity identified, this is surely the one which beckons as a promise rather than exists as a present reality.

The church's catholicity is nourished from below, draws on the rich and varied gifts of the community of faith, builds up Christians as lively stones in a spiritual house on the foundation of Christ and the apostles. Moreover, a church cannot be catholic unless it is prepared to receive, respect and draw into its life the contribution of every kind of believer and searcher.

The word "catholic" should be a disturbing one for authorities, both in church and state. Consider its implications. It points to the manifold resources of humanity, to the gifts of the Spirit distributed among the whole church, and to the manifold ministry which is to be developed from these gifts to produce a community's lively and rounded servant-existence in the world. Past ages and present ages need to contribute as do scientists, labourers, scholars, illiterates, poets and peasants. All the ends of the earth have seen the salvation of our God – so all the ends of the earth are called to contribute to theology and liturgy, and all cultures are called in freedom to work out indigenous forms of faith. A new way of handling power is proposed by Jesus. According to it, leadership will fall to women and children as readily as to men. Those regarded as slaves and weaklings in our present system, the marginalized in our societies and our churches, will be the ones who will be given honoured place, whose insights will count in the end. The last shall be the first and the first last.

* * *

The SCCs enlarge and enhance the concept of catholicity and offer this larger vision to the wider church.

The *contemporary extension of the church* in space could hardly have been imagined in Cyril's time, especially if we adopt the phrase of the New Delhi assembly "all in each place", which brings in not only the geographical location of people but their location in their culture, their faith and their sphere of human activity.

Church workers of various kinds have been sacrificially engaged in the shanty-towns and their equivalents for a long time. But a new thing is happening there. Through the development of SCCs people who felt that they were discards of society, good-for-nothings, failures, are realizing their worth in God's sight, whoever and wherever they are; they are learning to respect their own thinking, their own perceptions of life, their own gifts for prayer and worship, their own ability to interpret God's word in the Bible and to act accordingly, their own calling to change the world towards God's justice in face of all the powers to which they had previously been subservient. The SCCs are the right size for their thinking to be heard and, where need be, given critical appraisal – for providing also the support and love by which the members sustain one another.

The SCCs develop where they are, in terms of the situations in which they are embedded – and only then discover one another and reach out to one another. There is no model structure imposed from outside. So they can operate in a way which respects the culture in which they are set. When I was in China in 2001, I could understand the government's desire to have the Chinese Catholic churches sever their connection with Rome. House churches and registered churches, in whatever tradition, should draw on their own culture and history, not conform to some foreign pattern. Their coming together will be all the richer in consequence. In relation to other faiths, all I can speak of is the SCCs' openness to and teachability before all ways of trying to make sense of life.

When it comes to spheres of human activity, the official church seems at times to forget that its concern should be the kingdom, the whole of life working according to God's purpose. A visit to Italy illustrated this.

Eleven representatives of British churches visited Livorno in May 1984, in the course of a series of contacts with Italian BCCs between Turin in the north and Naples in the south. The BCCs of Coteto and Luogo Pio, Livorno, formed the church there whose life we shared. Coteto takes the area in which it is set as its main sphere of action. Luogo Pio is more broadly involved in the city.

We visited the city council and were welcomed by a member of the communist party, Ivo del Greco, who greeted us in the name of the council. Thereafter, Maria Volpi, deputy director of cultural affairs, and Antonio Aldo informed us about the main issues which the council was facing.

At the community centre in the docks, we got details concerning the successful self-management of the docks by the work-force (communist-led), and heard about the spirit in which they had faced crises such as the development of "containerization".

We spent time with sixty women and men staging a sit-in in a factory, and heard about their struggle with industrial authorities.

We met workers made redundant who were redesigning a building to be a community centre, with particularly the needs of old people in the area in mind.

We heard about the weekly meeting of fifty to sixty parents of young drug addicts. These parents gather in Coteto to increase their sensitivity to the problem and strengthen one another in coping with it. We heard of the work of a therapeutic community which helps young people to get "unhooked" from drugs. We visited the site of a cooperative for washing council vehicles, developed on land bought from Livorno council. A work-place and cafeteria were also to be erected there. The chief aim of the project was that young addicts, once unhooked, could find a positive outlet for their energies.

"Kingdom" things, not "church" things filled our agenda in Livorno. The total explanation was that the BCCs introduced us to what they were engaged in. Had we gone as a church delegation to parish churches, it would almost certainly have been church committees and church organizations that we would have contacted, for one of the ways in which avoiding action is taken by the church on earth is the promotion of self-subsisting and parallel activities. Self-subsisting activities are designed to keep in being and ticking over a church which is in fact called to spend itself in love for the world.

Parallel activities often duplicate enterprises in the world which have a "kingdom" character, denying them needed reinforcement and constructive and critical insights.

Parallel activities hold a great attraction. They highlight concerns of the church, while allowing it to stay at a safe distance from the heat of the battle and in the company of the like-minded. In essence, what happens is that the church tries to offer a less raw and demanding way of being world than the world offers. But it is the world as it is that God loves and the world as it is that is offered for our obedience. The church robs itself of insights on how God is working in the world which can come only by breaking out of church circles and getting alongside concerned women and men who have no explicit Christian commitment. Only thus can ways of righteousness in the world's life be identified and ways of unrighteousness unmasked.

* * *

The church's *completeness of doctrine* is to be realized throughout history. It will be attained only at the end of time. But the SCCs make a contemporary contribution which is of great importance. It comes partly from educated people who have direct access to the scriptures and who no longer feel they need to sit at the feet of specialists, partly from illiterate or little educated people who see life "from the underside of history" and produce angles of perception different from those traditionally communicated. These can get them to the heart of doctrinal positions which were previously obscure.

On one occasion I was asked, at short notice, to contribute to a discussion on homelessness. I thought I would have a fresh look at Jesus' saying, "Foxes have holes, and birds of the air have nests; but the Son of Man has nowhere to lay his head" (Matt. 8:20). Only two commentaries were to hand at that time. I found that both scholars were absorbed in the question why the phrase "the Son of Man" was used. Imagine a shanty-town dweller examining the same passage – imagine his or her awe and comfort that the Son of God Most High should be prepared to accept such an insecure and deprived state of life, alongside the poorest. Those of us who are scholars often lack means for understanding features that can be appreciated by those for whom life is a constant struggle. Of such contributions Hugo Assmann, Brazilian liberation theologian, wrote:

> Texts produced are "historical instruments of struggle..." [W]hen much more relevant things happen in the life of people than are happening... in theology, it is a sign that their testimonies – fragmentary, provisional, without much abstract consistency – have a theological resonance greater than that of theological treatises.

We also have fresh doctrinal insights from previously neglected cultures. A Native American writes:

> If we have Bibles and communion, why do we need doctrine conceived in another civilization? Why should we need Augustine, Aquinas, Barth and Tillich, when in our own past we have Beyanawidah, Tecumseh, Quetzalcoatl and Chilan Balan?

Ed de la Torre, interviewed in a "safe house" in the Philippines in 1973 when on the run from the police, shared the following:

> One Christmas, a group of about a hundred farmers came up here to demand land from the government. We held a midnight mass. We were reflecting on what that meant, and I felt that one of them expressed it well when he said, "The Christian meaning of what we are doing is this, no? At the eucharist, we have only a few hosts, only a little bread, and we break it up and give it to each other. Why is this? It is really an act of the poor. There is not enough, that's why we break it up. If there were enough for all we would all get a whole piece."
>
> Another farmer's observation is even more profound: "Even if there is not enough, we will not follow the logic of the development economists who say, 'Let's first increase the GNP. Then, if there is not enough, we will make sure that we first feed those who are strong enough to work. Others can take their chance.' No! We won't postpone the sharing. There will not be enough for everyone but no one will have nothing. The whole point is not abundance or scarcity but that we share in a real celebration. We are not just going to glorify scarcity for scarcity's sake as more heroic. Even more importantly, we are to share what there is available in the period of poverty. What is most important is our solidarity."

There was no explicit reference in this to the last supper, but I think the farmer, in his own way, was articulating a very profound eucharist, which I personally could not achieve with all my priestly training.

* * *

Regarding *adaptation to the needs of every person*, the exclusion of women from major decision-making positions in the church, notable especially in some hierarchies, has been largely overcome. In SCCs, there is no barrier to their leadership and there are probably more women in leadership positions than men. However, there can still be relapses into traditionalist macho habits!

Children's needs are attended to. My wife and I attended the worship of the Surgeon SCC in France.

To start with, there were instrumental music and hymns and songs of a contemporary religious character. We then had a Bible reading, the story of the widow who kept harassing the judge until she got justice. The children in particular, with the priest acting as the unjust judge (no child would accept the role), made a dramatic presentation of this biblical parable. It was remembered that there was somewhere a Halloween mask of an old lady, and one of the children went and found it to take the part of the widow. Thereupon other children, determined not to be left out, went and got a mask of a dog, and a mask of an American Indian – so there had to be a dog in the story and a Native American amongst Jesus' disciples.

The parable was acted out. It was asked how it might be represented in a contemporary way. It was decided that the question of justice might be illustrated by miming a game of basketball. Accordingly, the children mimed a basketball game in which the referee turned a blind eye to fouls, ignoring the pleas of those offended against. This gave the children an idea of the essential meaning of the parable, particularly when one of the adults helped them to see that God expected them, in any situation, to keep fighting for justice and pleading for justice for themselves and for others. There were then prayers of approach to the eucharist, taken by the children. The priest himself took the short act of consecration. The bread and wine were shared among the adults and three of the children, the older ones remaining while the younger ones had gone off to play. There was the giving of the peace with embraces, kisses or handshakes. Further prayers were made by the children, and some hymns ended the service.

How are the needs attended to of those who find resources in their own culture which cry out for incorporation in worship? A Panamanian member of an SCC shared their experience:

> The basic liturgy we have is the liturgy in the different sections of the parish, which the people prepare themselves in small groups. It is here that the relationship of concern is established, together with a desire to praise. They deepen their understanding that, when a prayer is made, it is made to the Lord who is present, and the community must begin to look for ways to live it out. But the basic structure is rather classical. The main liturgical contribution of the people came about very, very slowly – it was something indigenous. Some of the men in the community who played the guitar and drum, or the local folk instrument, the *bocina*, felt that the music they were singing in liturgical services wasn't really theirs. Their music was basically very simple dance music, but music which called for creation and participation. So they began to choose folk melodies that came from their grandfathers and their great-grandfathers, and to pick out different sounds that would express basic ideas – penitence, for instance.
>
> In the *Misa Tipica*, in "Lord have mercy", there is a kind of yodel called the *Saloma* which plaintively expresses the deep cry of need, of pain – the need for change and pain that things don't change. The response to this cry is "Glory to the Lord!" The understanding of the people is that the cry of pain brings an immediate answer from the Lord who lives in pain, who is here in the midst of change. When one realizes that the Lord is present with one in it all, one has immediate reason to rejoice.

We asked if people danced in any of the liturgies.

> Yes, on special occasions, at the offering of the gifts. What happens is that there is a moment in the liturgy where the people

say, "We want to give something; what is the thing that is most ours?" Well, it's dance. So a couple or a group will dance as a presentation, to make an offering. This happens for instance at the feast of the resurrection of the Lord. At Christmas, it is done in a sort of pageant. The people work out different reactions to the reality of the incarnation according to their own rural folk tradition. After the reading of the gospel, there is a presentation of gifts to the Lord who is one with them again. It takes the form of a dance.

We had a marriage here at Pentecost. Pentecost is a great feast; it is actually the *fiesta* of the patron of our church. We did not want to march around with statues of saints – it is hard to have the Holy Spirit incarnate in a piece of wax! But we had a wedding – a young couple who could dance very well. They decided to get married in rural costume, their real dress. They danced the offertory. It was beautiful, because it really expressed what they felt towards each other; and in their faces, in their way of dancing, you could see the desire to create together. The coming of the Spirit became vivid through their own relationship, their relationship to the people, their offering of both to God.

What kind of church has adapted its life of faith to a revolution and its aftermath? Listen to the response of a Nicaraguan SCC. New hymns were called for!

The revolution was such a deliverance! It gave us fresh insights into the exodus. We needed to give praise to the Lord for our new-found freedom. We then had to face the hostility of the USA to that freedom, the destruction and death produced by the CIA's Contra army. At that point, we needed other kinds of songs, such as those of the Israelites who wandered in the wilderness and were never sure of what lay ahead. We needed music and words to hold up to God all that we had come through – to the God in whom we trust who met us in a fresh way in our history.

The Wild Goose resource group of the Iona community in Scotland has played a notable part not only in providing new words and music for liturgies but for sharing widely, throughout the world, songs and stories coming from many countries and cultures.

* * *

As for *the church's perfection of spiritual grace and power* I can only point to the modest claims of the SCCs. They do not present themselves as an alternative church or as the original church reconstituted in our time. They simply claim to be "a way of being church". There is spiritual grace and power in the modesty of the claim.

5. The Marks of the Church: Apostolic

The message from the sixth assembly of the World Council of Churches at Vancouver in 1983 includes the following words: "We renew our commitment to mission and evangelism. By this we mean that *deep identification with others* in which we can tell the good news..." The words reveal awareness of the apostolic nature of the church's commission. The word "apostolic" is often generally and vaguely equated by Protestants with "missionary" and/or "evangelistic". But the word has its own weight.

In the original Greek it is used to describe seafaring expeditions, especially military ones. It has the connotation of "sending-in-order-to-attain-an-objective" (to engage an enemy fleet, to found a colony or such), a flavour which another word for send, *pempein*, lacks. Within this framework of meaning, the emphasis is firmly on the act of sending and being sent. Those who are sent may not even know the kind of assignment which awaits them. They are under command. They will get their sealed orders in due course. In this way, the apostle is to be distinguished from the envoy who has a clear charge to fulfil, or a message to convey.

The word is used also in relation to the divine commissioning of a human being to act as a *kataskopos*, i.e. as someone who goes where wanted and feels the pulse of ongoing life there, all eyes and ears, alert to register how human beings are managing their affairs. The work of the *episkopos* is open only to those who have fulfilled the primary function of being *kataskopos*.*

The writer of Hebrews speaks of Jesus as our "Apostle and High Priest". Jesus was, during almost the whole of his life-time, a *kataskopos* located in the thick of life, drinking in all that was going on around him, learning people's manifold earthy languages, sharing their daily life with its ups and downs, sharpening his judgment on a basis of deep knowledge of "what was in everyone" (John 2:24,25). This qualified him to be our *episkopos* (Heb. 4:14-16). He was

---

* Gerhard Kittel, *Theological Dictionary of the New Testament*, Grand Rapids MI, Eerdmans, 1965, vol. 2.

uniquely Apostle and High Priest. The apostle is one who is sent and available, who digs into situations and waits there at the ready. He or she can be kept on the sidelines as long as God chooses, thrown into battle when God judges the time ripe, given instructions as the battle proceeds. In Gethsemane, Jesus' "nevertheless not my will but yours be done" was the word of God's apostle, in the right place at the right time but sweating great drops of blood to know and to do the will of the Father.

In the book of the Acts, the life of St Paul illustrates features of apostleship. In the church at Antioch, a group given to prayer and fasting are told by the Holy Spirit, "Set apart Barnabas and Saul for the work to which I have called them." There is no identification of the work. It may lead them into strange territory. It is for the Spirit to say (13:1,2). Moreover it may seem to thwart their very calling. In Acts 16:6-15, the Holy Spirit forbids Paul to proclaim the gospel in Asia, or even to enter Bithynia. It is because Paul is obedient to the prompting of the Spirit that, in a dream, he is invited to go to Macedonia; and from Philippi he begins his share in the European mission. Luke 9:13 describes other features of apostleship. Disciples go exposed and vulnerable into strange situations. Only if they take that risk will they find what God has in store for them. It will be impossible from safe ground to anticipate their assignments.

The Twelve fulfilled a representative function in the foundation of the New Israel and were without successors. The idea that they had successors is a theory promoted late in history, clearly designed to strengthen the status of the ordained. The significant number 12 was first retained by means of the appointment of Matthias to fill Judas' place; then the whole situation was prized open by Paul in his apostleship; before long, the word "apostle" was adopted for many who were active in the young church as it reached into strange places or was sent helter-skelter by persecution across the ancient world. It is clear from 2 Corinthians 11:13 and First Thessalonians 2:6 that this is so, but especially in First Corinthians 15:5,7 where Paul speaks of the appearance of the risen

Christ "to the twelve... then to all the apostles". The apostolic calling has become a mark of the church – ordained and lay, women and men, children and the old, slaves and slave-girls being open, as was Paul, to be called to be apostles of Jesus Christ.

Apostleship: being where it matters

Women are included in the apostolic calling of the whole Christian community. Indeed the women who testified to Christ risen from the dead are the commanding sign of the character which apostleship has to bear from the time of the resurrection forward. Before then, the number 12 provided a link with the 12 tribes of the old dispensation and formed a statement that the work of Jesus was not to discard but to transform the old. The Twelve represented Israel as bearing a promise for the whole world (cf. Gen. 11). They were primary sources, as those who "had been with Jesus". The continuity of Jesus' life with God's action in the past was thus affirmed and symbolized. The women at the cross and at the tomb formed a "sign forward", a sign that all peoples and all kinds of people are now called to share in Christ's ministry. Jesus' sending out of the Twelve had heralded a faith which would be for the whole world.

That world dimension was made even more explicit when the Seventy went out in mission (Luke 10). Seventy was believed to be the number of nations inhabiting the earth. What the women at the tomb now made clear was that, from the time of the resurrection, apostleship becomes a mark of the life of the whole church. The women were found where it mattered – by the cross and at the tomb, *kataskopoi*. In the course of fulfilling the normal duties which fell to women, the anointing of the body, they came up against a new reality. Events proved that they bore a constitutive hallmark of apostleship – the readiness for unexpected orders. So to them was entrusted the primary announcement of an astounding new fact. It was due to their faithfulness in apostleship, in going where they were sent, available there, that they became the first evangelists of the new dispensation.

The word "apostolic" retains the sense of physical movement, adds to that a movement of directed energy, entails movement into fresh geographical, cultural, class, racial fields. It can convey to us today a sense of leaving behind church-premises activities and being available in unfamiliar discovery-situations; of breaking away from known and familiar company to establish relationships with those who are in some kind of foreign territory; of being ready not only to be used to convert others but to be converted to new appreciations of God's large work in the world – as Peter the believer was converted at the hands of Cornelius the enquirer. The word implies that research and analysis should be treated as necessary disciplines to accompany commitment. Those who would be disciples are required to be teachable before the world as it faces them in that particular time and place in which God has entrusted to them the gift of life (John 1:12,13). It is in an instructed way that they are to play their part in his transforming purpose, as those who know the scene in which they are set.

The word "apostle" is a word of great courtesy and tenderness. It carries with it a sense of deep respect for other people, as and where they are; it honours their way of life, their insights, their native manner of expressing themselves and seeks to understand and value these; it requires people to move from where they are to where these differences can be appreciated. It denotes a sensitivity which characteristically waits for invitation, refusing to proceed roughshod into other places and other lives. It requires the believer to be open to further conversion – often coming from unlikely sources. It is a word which clarifies the distinction between evangelizing and proselytizing.

Small wonder that, in Argentina, in our time, the word *misión* with its memory of the *conquistadores* coming with a Bible in one hand and a sword in the other is being replaced by *caminando* – walking together. Those who walk together need not be converted one to the other: they can both be converted to the truth.

The SCCs know what it is to be required to go into strange territory where they are not sure of their footing. When I served in Selly Oak Colleges, I came across the following example contrasting SCCs' awareness of an apostolic calling with that of the traditional church.

At San Martín, near Barcelona, people from basic Christian communities asked me about Selly Oak, Birmingham. I told them of the nearness of Longbridge, the Austin Motors works down the road. They were immediately interested and asked me when there was a dispute at that works how the churches in that locality reacted. Did they mainly take the side of the work-force or of the management? I had to confess that they took very little direct interest as congregations in any industrial dispute. They said,

> Oh, come on! We know that there will be different reactions in different circumstances. Most times we need to side with the work-force. When there is a dispute, there is usually some real injustice at the root of it and the work-force are those who take the brunt. There are times when we should side with the management because they seem to have a point to which the work-force are a bit blind.
>
> In each case, one of our jobs, as Christians, is to keep the one side open to the other. If you take the side of the shop-floor workers, your identification with them includes the business of communicating to them something which belongs to the management's view of things. If you believe that the management are in the right, you encourage them to appreciate how the shop-floor workers are placed, and how they are reacting. But you always need to take sides and not sit on the fence. Of course, there has to be a good foundation from which to act. You have to build up an understanding of the development of industry in your area over a period of many years. It takes time and energy. All that we are asking is whether the churches in the area of Longbridge usually come out on the side of the work-force or of the management.

I had to repeat my point about the church's indifference. They shook their heads, incredulous. "How can people claim to be Christians and stay out of such things?" they asked.

For Baptists in Rome, the formation of SCCs in common with Roman Catholics involved going beyond traditional ways of interpreting the scriptures. A Baptist pastor gave an account of their experience as follows:

> We Baptists give great honour to the Bible. We tend to assume that it contains all that matters. So we would gather round it and dig into it repeatedly. After some time, it became clear to us that we were giving no significant testimony, making no impact on the life of the neighbourhood.
>
> At that point, we noticed Roman Catholic groups which were certainly making an impact. We had just enough courage – in spite of the dismissiveness and, at times, persecution which we had suffered at the hands of their church – to go to them and say, "We think you have found something in the Christian faith which we need, too." They gave us a warm welcome: "Join us!" they said, so we did. In no time at all they were saying to us, "You are so clued up on the Bible! We are ignoramuses. This is not one-way traffic, it is two-way!" We shared what each had found in the gospel, developing a dynamic relationship with one another and engaging in life in the world.

What difference did it make?

> The first thing was that we became aware of homeless people in our area. They had been there, right under our noses, but we had not noticed them. We then discovered that there was a problem of homelessness. People were not made homeless by chance or bad management of their resources but by the way "the system" worked. The root of the matter turned out to be city council priorities. We Baptists had to learn skills in city politics!

It became clear to us that concern for the kingdom of God requires us to give attention both to the faith and to the situations people face in the world. Some basic communities in Rome became merely biblicized or merely politicized. They soon went out of existence. Those which remain are convinced about the double reference of Christian discipleship. Christians must never retreat into the Bible or retreat into politics.

* * *

The crossing of frontiers at the command of the Holy Spirit is costly, as a small community in Peru and as the Sojourners community in the USA have testified.

In 1972, challenged by Jesus' example, ten young people in Lima, Peru, who had trained as teachers and could have been upwardly mobile, decided to live in a deprived community. They put down roots into the life of the people, accepted their culture, learnt their key words and used these to encourage the development of awareness of their oppressed situation and to encourage choices for freedom. Four of the teachers took on paid employment. The $72 per month earned by the four had to support the total team and pay for teaching materials and apparatus as well. They crossed a financial frontier, adopting a simple style of living that allowed the income of a few to do for all. Thus they found an alternative to that of financing by outside agencies.

They also crossed an educational frontier, immersing themselves among those who had little education or none, honouring their wisdom, enlarging it. They crossed a class frontier, refusing the status available to middle-class professionals, choosing rather to live alongside those who were regarded as belonging to the lowest stratum of society. They crossed a cultural frontier, deliberately refusing to be cultural capitalists, deciding to honour the culture of the lowly rather than the prestige culture for which they could have opted. They crossed a frontier of individualism, for they acted as a team. Four of them came to meet me to make it clear that leadership does not fall to any one of them, but is shared. I asked them about the denominational rooting of their small community. "We are just Christians," they replied. "It is the Christian faith which is at the back of what we do."

Jim Wallis spoke of the experience of the Sojourners community in the USA:

> I think there is tremendous pressure – cultural, economic, political pressure – that people who choose this life come under in the US. We are such a minority; and to live by the gospel in this culture inevitably marginalizes you culturally, politically and economically. And you don't feel like you're part of a movement that is reshaping your country and your world and your history – as, I imagine, you do if you're in Brazil and you're in one of 80,000 basic communities, and you are poor and the majority are

poor, and you feel like you are participating in something that really is a new reformation in the church and a whole new social revolution in that society. There, while you may be poor, while you may be suffering, you have a sense of being part of something that is historically significant and is changing the face of your society and your world and your history.

That is not something that we feel in North America. Mostly people feel small and ineffectual and marginalized, and that's truly what we are. There is a movement in the churches, it's very strong, and it has been an obstacle, a point of resistance to the government, and we're in the middle of all of that: and yet we haven't won any political battle whatsoever. We have maybe been a thorn in their side. We have been a community of resistance. We've been a problem for them, for we're under a lot of surveillance. A lot of our people have been in jail, all the time now all over the country.

But you don't have the feeling that you're on the edge, on the brink of any sweeping changes either in the church or in society. That really must push you back to basic things like faithfulness being more important than effectiveness. That's true, but I think for many people it's hard to live that way, and to maintain that, particularly over the long haul. People can do that for a few years, five years, maybe ten. But to live their lives this way requires a depth of faith. It requires a broader global analysis where you can feel yourself to be part of something around the world, so that you feel linked to what's happening in the Philippines and in South Africa and in Brazil.

In Sojourners' case, we have such deep personal friendships and relationships with people around the world – that's a lot of what sustains me. It's in those connections where I feel that our part right now is to be a movement, really a movement in resistance to the power system of the United States, which is indeed the enemy of those movements around the world. I'm not speaking here always of the kind of overt, visible persecution and repression that's easier to see, because I think persecution in that way sometimes strengthens and purges belief and builds up the body of Christ. The greater enemy to faith than persecution is seduction.

* * *

It was with their hearts in their mouth that, under the leadership of Helen Steven and Ellen Moxley, members of the Iona community family groups (their SCCs) opposed the Trident nuclear submarines. They did not know what they were letting themselves in for – jail certainly, but maybe the ire of the locals for whom the Faslane development had meant jobs and a secure income. Ellen was one of the three who got into one security area and destroyed a substantial amount of equipment, tipping it into the loch. They were jailed on remand, tried – and found not guilty since they were attempting to prevent the criminal deployment of weapons of mass destruction! Though this judgment was legally reversed some time later, it remained a famous victory.

We twice tried without success to make contact with small Christian communities meeting in the underground in Hungary during the communist years. We knew they were there, much as astronomers knew of the existence of a planet on which they could not yet train telescopes, alerted by disturbance in the sky around. We had to be very sensitive in our approach, otherwise we could have brought the secret police down on them.

Three months after my wife's death in 1987, I tried again. This time I was put in touch with 6000 small communities who had been meeting clandestinely out of sight of the communist regime. My next contact was after the Velvet Revolution, at a day conference. I found that the 5000 communities in the Roman Catholic tradition and the 1000 communities in various Protestant traditions had made common cause and were now operating in five networks. The day was entirely devoted to identifying social and political engagements which they had not been able to undertake when the secret police had been ready to pounce on any public manifestation. They knew that such commitments belonged to a full expression of faith. Once the opportunity was offered, they were quick to seize it.

This joining together of things which had become separated – prayer and politics, work and worship, the evangelical, the economic and the ecumenical (the Trident protests embraced all kinds of responsible groups, not just Christian) marks the apostolic character and quality of the life of SCCs.

6. The Marks of the Church: Church

From the beginning of the life of the church, it is made clear that the Christian community is not to be classified as a religious society. Words for religious societies were available in Greek, ready for the adopting. One could have been selected, filled out and given new dimensions of meaning. *Thiasos* lays emphasis mainly on celebrating and praising together. *Eranos* and *koinonia* place the emphasis on fellowship, including fellowship round a meal. *Synodos* is used of a company of people following a common way. In light of the Old Testament background, the word *synagoge* would appear to have been likeliest of all. Why was it rejected? It referred particularly and concretely to the Jewish community meeting in religious assembly. Also, in time, it came to refer to the building rather than the people (the word *kuriakon*, from which we get "kirk" and "church", also emphasizes building rather than people).

The word *ecclesia* was chosen (Matt. 16:18 and 18:17; twenty-three times by Luke and it is the norm in Paul's epistles). *Ecclesia* is a word for calling out or summoning. It is almost equivalent to "a call-up" and is used for the mustering of an army. But it also describes the assembling of free citizens for regular or emergency meetings on important public issues such as changes in the law, matters of war and peace, treaties, budgets, appointments to official positions. Major matters which affected the whole community formed the agenda of such an "ecclesial gathering".

Meetings opened with prayers and sacrifices to the gods. Every citizen had a right to speak. If weighty decisions needed to be made, these could not be put to the vote until experts had first been called in to make their contribution. The mind of the people and the advice of specialists informed one another. Adequately instructed decisions could then be made.

Ecclesia kept the sense of *people together* rather than of a building in which they could meet; it retained the dynamic of *tackling unfinished business* rather than giving a sense of observing ceremonial routines; and it implied summoning a *public gathering about public concerns* rather than religious people meeting for religious purposes (note the unself-conscious use of the word in Acts 19:32,39,41 where the idea of "church" is quite missing). That the word *ecclesia* was adopted for the church implies that Jesus' life, death and resurrection are to be treated as a public event, witnessed to publicly. They form a matter of public importance, placed before the public, inviting a response from all sorts of people, not just from the religiously minded.

The church contradicts its own nature when it acts as a religious society or club. It contradicts its own nature when its concerns are internal to itself and fail to embrace the aspirations, sufferings, joys, cries and crises of humanity. It contradicts its own nature when it ceases to be a fount of new life and of daring enterprise.

Paul teams up the word *ecclesia* with *soma* (body) and *oikos* (building). The church is the "body of Christ" (see esp. Rom. 12:5ff., 1 Cor. 12:12ff.) comprising tissues, organs, limbs which contribute and receive within a common life. It is the "building of God" made up of lively stones with the apostles the foundation and Jesus Christ the chief corner or coping stone; a "spiritual house" (1 Pet. 2:5, 1 Tim. 3:15), a "temple" (1 Cor. 3:16,17; 2 Cor. 6:16; Eph. 2:21). The *charismata*, the gifts of the Spirit, are distributed among the people to equip Christ's body for tasks God assigns. Every baptized person is equipped for ministry. (The *charismata* cannot confidently be restricted even to believers. Enquirers, doubters, stated unbelievers may be spirit-gifted...)

Among the people are distributed skills for leadership and organization, healing, for developing fresh languages of faith, for discernment of spirits. When particular functions are fulfilled by particular members, these do not elevate any above others, for it is the people together who are the "body" and the "building". Jesus seems deliberately to have entrusted the coming of his kingdom on earth to a motley crew, common people who as Mark 12:37 says, heard him "with delight", of whom Jesus himself said, they "heard not the voice of strangers".

The over-use in church history of the idea of shepherd and sheep has resulted in the elevating of clergy and the devaluing of the rest of the membership. The image has been used to assert power positions on the part of some over others. Shepherds do not always bear a good image in the scriptures. They can be neglectful, exploiting the flock for their own purposes, employing ruthless severity to get their will obeyed – see Isaiah 56:9-12; Jer. 23:1,2; Ezek. 34:1-10; Zech. 10:3, 11:5. "Hirelings" was Jesus' word for such keepers of sheep (John 10:1-13). "It shall not be so among you," said Jesus of domination of that kind.

Members of the one body

Scripturally, Jesus is the one shepherd, and he ratifies his vocation by giving his life for the sheep (so martyrs really can be shepherds). Others are, at best, "under-shepherds", "feeders of the flock", words which carry no status implications. It is a whole people, *laos*, who were left to be the sign, instrument and foretaste of what God had in mind for all humanity. There was no priestly caste in the church. Converted priests became members of the *laos*. It was presbyters whom Paul and Barnabus appointed to take oversight in congregations: the word *hiereus* (mediating priest) simply was not used for leaders in the young church.

Every member has a place and function indispensable to the life of the whole church both in its local and universal expressions. Every member, from baptism, has a work of testimony to offer in action and word which, by virtue of its relevance in local situations, contributes to the whole church's testimony to the whole world in all ages. Every member has a contribution to make in building up worship by concretely contributing out of one time and place to that worship which continues throughout and beyond time in the communion of saints.

Local churches drawing on their particular histories and facing particular situations in particular cultures can recognize themselves to be "outcrops of one rock" (as P.T. Forsyth puts it). Christ can then be presented to the world in his richness and fullness (Eph. 1:22,23). His relevance to every situation can be brought home to people where they live and work, for it is there that his body will be found. Local churches, faithful where they are, will keep discovering new dimensions of discipleship as they grow up in Christ (Eph. 4:16). These insights they may contribute to the larger church, receiving, in return, what will sustain, enlarge and correct their life. Thus, all are built up in unity and in love.

There is no need to preserve such a church or to secure its future. Top-heavy institutional means, geared to achieving this end, simply make past practice the pattern for the shape of the church in the unknown territory which lies ahead and prevent it from meeting Christ as he comes from the future with new gifts in his torn hands.

The heart of the matter is put succinctly in Eph. 5:29: "For no one ever hates his own body, but he nourishes and tenderly cares for it, just as Christ does for the church, because we are members of his body." Jesus Christ's word to those who are anxious about the survival of the church is, "Relax. Leave to me what is my own business."

"It is for both religious and social reasons that an oppressed and scattered population comes together to form an 'ecclesia'... People come together regularly to think about common problems in the light of the faith, to pray and to act," said Clovis Boff, drawing on his Latin American experience of SCCs where he worked part of the year in the fields alongside Native Americans. SCCs are church in a way which reminds official, traditional churches of features of their life which need to be given fresh attention.

There is "the public gathering for public concerns". Edmund Arens gave details of actions taken by the Frankfurt SCCs, speaking in 1984:

> Last November, we organized a kind of penance walk under the biblical motto "Guide our feet into the way of peace" (from Luke). We asked a lot of other basic communities and other church communities in Frankfurt and the surrounding area to go with us on this walk. We wanted to articulate through public expression our concern with the peace question, and to do this

in a quite liturgical way – that's to say, in a penance walk with several stopping points in churches where we had acts of worship, and in front of the buildings of bodies which have relations to the governments engaged in the arms race; for example, in front of the US consulate and in front of the Soviet mission. There we had acts of worship and also handed in letters for Andropov and Reagan in which we demanded disarmament, a decision not to station the cruise and Pershing missiles on our soil, and to withdraw the SS20s from the GDR, from Czechoslovakia and other Eastern European countries.

I think to walk about 15 kms under a cross, to walk in silence, to sing liturgical songs, to read biblical texts, to pray, to have speeches, to meditate – that's all a kind of worship; it is political worship.

The participation of the Iona community in anti-Trident demonstrations has been mentioned. There are many, many more comparable actions by SCCs.

These are signs that the SCCs do not come under the bracket of religious societies or clubs. When we took part in the first European congress of SCCs, initiated by the Dutch in 1983, we were allocated to the Salland community. It had come into being though a wide invitation. A man or woman, I am not sure which, had phoned a few acquaintances and had put an advertisement in the local paper saying something like this: "I want to find what it is to live the Christian life today. I think that the official church is hindering rather helping me. Anyone care to join me in finding how to live Christian life today?" In no time, thirty people had come together. By the time we got there, this had risen to more than seventy and the group had to divide into two for the sake of efficiency. The dynamic power of this form of meeting is clear from the following extracts from notes I made as I visited home churches in ten centres around Australia in 1990:

I think there are two sorts of people in the groups: there are those who have become completely dissatisfied with what was happening in the official church and have left for that reason; then there are those who are refugees from the institutional church, who have been really hurt by it, who are looking for some place to be where they can be loved. They have been treated, I would say, in one way or another, as people who have not come up to scratch and they are looking for acceptance; they gravitate towards this kind of group knowing that people will not stand in judgment on them but accept them as they are...

You can be anonymous in the traditional church: just go and nothing else. I quite enjoy going to a good Anglican service with a lovely liturgy, but for the day-to-day nitty-gritty of life I find it meaningless. In this community, even the last couple of months have made a big difference to our lives. Our children from an early age had been happily in a community, and before we dragged them to church very much against their will. Today I wanted to come on my own to the community, but when the children heard it was to be a house church event, they insisted on coming. They love it.

Over the last twenty years, I've had many complicated things to work my way through and I find that in the home church people stick by me, and it is really church to me. I see the Holy Spirit somehow networking through all these people, and this has been especially clear to me in a difficult time I had to cope with recently. A part of the network which is in Brisbane actually helped me considerably as well as the members in Canberra.

I'm Charles, and Doris and I came from South Africa 15 years ago. We were quite happy in the institutional church, but I was sick at the time and couldn't do with crowds, which prevented my going to church, and somebody pointed us in this direction. I wasn't too sure of it all, but they were quite happy that we should just come and have a look. We found the group totally accepting and loving and they placed no obligations upon us to continue with them. It was the most wonderful experience. We felt we had come home. We can see that this is in line with New Testament practice, but we still have no dispute with the institutional church as it is.

One person spoke of

the experience that my wife and I had in working through the death of our marriage, drawing upon the strength of this group to go into the deepest strains and feelings – that was what began to enable us to find our way through, to the experience of forgiveness and new life on the other side of the death. I'll never forget that – it was an experience of really being the church.

About 13 or 14 years ago, I had major surgery and spent a year in my bedroom isolated. I had gone to an Anglican church before that. That experience disillusioned me, and I felt that I would never belong to anything like that again. Friends here, whom we knew from Scripture Union camps, invited us to come to a home church group. I was so weak that I could only lie on the floor in terrible pain. In addition, we had a profoundly deaf child who was also hyperactive – so we did not fit into the normal scheme of things for the traditional church, where people kept saying how well they coped. I think that being loved in that group got me back on my feet and walking around.

As for the church as a building, the media so often try to estimate the strength of the church in relation to church attendance. Some years ago when I was at Fuller Theological Seminary, California, students approached me wearing T-shirts which said "Don't Go To Church". When you looked after them, the message on the back was "Be The Church". If the church is to be like salt and leaven, it is its life and penetrative quality which matter. Bishop Fridolin Zahradnik of the clandestine church in Czechoslovakia has testified to the power of the mass when held in houses rather than cathedrals and the greater impact produced by the ordination of priests and the consecration of bishops if that took place in workshops rather than ecclesiastical buildings.

Bishop Patrick Kalilombe, speaking about BCCs in Africa at the School of Oriental and African Studies in London in 1985, pointed out the irrelevance of much that was exported from churches in the West to other parts of the world. He hazarded that the larger proportion of finance injected into churches in many African countries from rich churches in the West had no relevance other than a negative one to the style of life and Christian witness of the recipients. He reflected on the position of a bishop in particular:

Who needs a cathedral? A meeting place is enough. Who needs a palace? A house like anyone else's suffices. Who needs a Mercedes Benz? To be able to get around is enough. Who needs expensive training? It may simply prove a handicap, preventing people from appreciating the resources within their own cultures, the gifts of their own people, the methods of gaining knowledge and handling life which have been tried and trusted through centuries.

Among images for the church, Paul especially emphasizes that of a body, with all the limbs and organs interacting to sustain its life and move it forward, none with greater or less importance than another. Is anything less like a body than a hierarchy?

I have a remedy to the problem of hierarchy where SCCs are made the basic constitutive element in the life of the church – in Mexico, in the diocese of Mendez Arceo; in Adelaide, Australia; in Czechoslovakia in the "Church of Silence"; and, especially, in the diocese of Ipil, Mindanao, in the Philippines.

Listen to the delight and surprise in the voice of a medical missionary sister interviewed on tape at Alicia, Mindanao. She had been serving outside her country for ten years, and was not long back. The occasion was the prelature assembly, in which met about 120 representatives from the Roman Catholic diocese of Ipil.

> When I left these people would have been cowed and voiceless in any assembly of this kind. They would have accepted that it was their superiors who had the right to tell them what to do and think, and they would not have dared raise a word in protest. But what have we here? Bishop Escaler is not even taking the chair – it is a young layman who guides the assembly, with the bishop contributing from time to time with the others. Women with families, fishermen, landless labourers, young people are making thoughtful and articulate contributions. They listen carefully to others and take their own share in trying to discern the will of God for the diocese. And their sense of dignity before God, their confidence, their determination – all spring from their faith! Many times they are afraid, as they experience the violence and destructiveness which they meet in daily experience. But they stand, and they stand together.

Imagine a pyramid. Turn it into a spiral. Then press it down. It becomes a spring. Four times per year that spring was tightened in Ipil with pressure coming from local situations right to the prelature assembly. The spring then wound back to the local scenes, communicating a vision by means of dynamic tension. What is more, this process overcame the remoteness of the higher echelons of hierarchy because women and men in local leadership positions were drawn in to the prelature assembly so that the flavour of what was happening at the grassroots could be retained throughout. I recorded at the time:

> The basis of it all is 1200 cells in which representatives of six to eight families meet, every week, for evaluation of their situation and a search for biblical resources to deal with it. Each Sunday, the insights and questions of these cells are drawn into an act of eucharistic worship, conducted in almost every instance by a local lay leader, with a reserved sacrament. These local leaders meet once every month in "zones" for about two days, to reflect critically on the adequacy of their own forms of leadership and on their understanding of the Bible, so that they may be effective facilitators of the whole dynamic process.
>
> Every second month, a representative from each zone and the presidents of chapel worship take part in a parish meeting which offers a broader overview of the church's tasks and provides opportunity for news and exchange of information. A district meets four times a year, and each district gathers together the thinking and concerns of four parishes and feeds these into the prelature assembly which gathers up contributions from the life of the whole diocese and offers representatives of the whole diocese the opportunity to work them through. Fresh insights then go back through the various channels, right back to the local situation, fructifying the new life. This structure is still called "hierarchical". The word, I suppose, may continue to be used – but I would call it a "pulse of life" structure which draws blood from the outermost parts of the body of Christ through various channels to the heart where it is purified and recirculated through the body.

So the church grows in faith, from the roots up.

In my Reformed tradition (the Church of Scotland identifies itself as "Catholic and Reformed"), the image of shepherd and sheep has been only too powerful. "The minister" has been thought of rather like the axle of a wheel which is always at the centre of things and holds everything together. Services are most often one-man-band or one-woman-band affairs with the congregation dumbed down or given minor parts to play. This is in sharp contrast to a service in the early church described in first Corinthians 14:26-33 which is marked by the full participation of members. Paul does not try to thwart that building up of worship from the congregation as a whole. He simply insists that it must be orderly. Moreover, he starts not with an "if you should meet in this way" or "when you might meet in this way": he uses the word *hotan* – "*whenever* you meet...", indicating that the normal form of worship is fully participatory.

Go to worship in Iona abbey. The service might be led by a professor of theology, or a cook, or a gardener, or a housekeeper or a maintenance man. The main structure of worship will have been hammered out by representatives of the SCCs or family groups. Space is still left for those with different tasks to build into it the concerns, hopes, longings, praises which derive from their particular experiences.

* * *

I go to Iglesia la Merced in Nicaragua. The worship leader has a roving microphone. When it comes to prayers, members of the congregation will suggest people and events, or ask for the microphone and offer the prayer directly. When it comes to the sermon, it is the whole congregation which builds it up. This is not superficial, off-the-top-of-the-head stuff. Seven SCCs form the congregation. They have met during the week, shared their knowledge of who and what should be prayed for, worked on the scriptural material, gained insights to contribute – and come equipped to build up worship. Ephesians 4:16 speaks of Christ "from whom the whole body, joined and knit together by every ligament with which it is equipped, as each part is working properly, promotes the body's growth in building itself up in love". You can see that growth taking place in the participatory worship of SCCs.

I have noticed a strange debate recently which turns reality on its head. It concerns the question of whether the word "ministry" should be used only of the ordained. The reality is that those of us who are ordained have to cherish the gifts of the Spirit and release the ministries of the whole church. The experience of SCCs in Panama put things right side up:

> We find people taking on themselves a ministry based on what has been their own personal experience of resurrection in a particular area of their life. For instance, Fidel Gonzales is extremely adept at talking to people who are sick and dying, who need someone to put an element of hope in their lives. Fidel is good at this because he himself has twice been close to death. A car turned over and he was almost killed. His brain was badly damaged; one side was knocked out, and the doctors thought he wouldn't be able to speak. However, he is left-handed, and as there is some kind of relationship between the right side of the brain and the left side of the body, so he came out of it. It was an experience of resurrection for him. Slowly he learned to walk again, to write again. To hear him talk about his own experience, or talk to a person about what sickness implies, what death and the resurrection mean, is a fantastic experience because *it is something that he has lived*. He can fulfil ministry in this particular way.
>
> Favio and Adelina are a couple who have lived out the difficulties of marriage. This is a second marriage for Adelina. The first was an absolute disaster. To find in a marriage relationship what she has found with Favio! Then to see what Favio has become! Here is a man who stutters badly, and all of a sudden there he is, standing up and performing a liturgy of the word, giving communion to an area group! This all comes out of the reality of resurrection in marriage, resurrection in a portion of life which they have lived out together. Hear Favio talk to a young couple who are going to he married – this man who really couldn't speak before: "Now look, marriage is a completely different experience, nobody can tell you what it is going to be like. It is going to be yours. You must put the elements of creativity in it." To listen to him speak to those about to be married is something to live for!
>
> You find in the group people who have a clear vision of where we should be going. Chado is recognized not only in San

Miguelito but by the laymen in all Panama as the person they most want to listen to, and to tell their troubles to, and to have him say where we are all going. He has a tendency to shy away from this, he is afraid of this kind of power. But if there is a man with the ability and the vision of bishop in Panama, he is the one.

* * *

We have developed, along the way, a false idea of church and ministry. We need to take a different path. We have to be prepared to listen to the Flemish Dominican theologian Edward Schillebeeckx who, in an address to the congress of ministries in April 1979, said:

If one places oneself in the perspective of the ancient church (the first thousand years) in terms of ecclesiology and ministry, then what one calls today a lack of priests will seem to derive from causes which are not linked to ministry itself. Notably, these causes are the conditions of admission to ministry which have been imposed during the course of history, for reasons which are not specifically ecclesiological. There are more than enough Christian women and men who possess the necessary charisma in terms of the theology of the church and ministry – such as, for example, many catechists in Africa, workers who are pastoral animators in Europe and elsewhere...: taking account of the canons of the ancient church, they match up to all requirements.

7. A Forward Look

Within God's transforming purpose for the creation, people are called to collaborate as fellow-workers with Jesus Christ. One of the challenges is to reshape the church so that it becomes more truly what it is called to be.

One of the first things to acknowledge in the West is our indebtedness to the past and especially to three kinds of people. There have been those who, faced with the inadequacies of the church as they found it, made the best of what was there and invested imagination, skill and energy – so that the water of life still reached people even though it was through leaky buckets. There have been those who found church-as-is so unlike church-as-called-to-be that out of integrity they broke away (as one SCC put it, "life was somewhere else"), producing a useful crisis which shook the foundations of the existing church. There have been those who remained on the fringes, seeking meaning for life, asking awkward questions, making us think twice about our priorities and styles of life.

We may be fortunate in the West in having this sense of crisis. The church catholic may be helped if we deal with it constructively.

Unwillingness to change

The real problem does not lie in the church's inadequacies. Every institution experiences these during its life and needs reform. The problem lies in unwillingness to change at a time when it is becoming clear that adjustments will not be enough. Drastic change is required.

In the Reformed tradition in which I was brought up, A.C. Craig saw the establishment of Scottish Churches House, an interchurch conference and retreat centre, as a great ecumenical step forward. He was asked to take retreats for clergy there. He testified wearily to what he found. To start with, the vision of a church as it might become gripped people. At the last session participants looked again at the task they would return to and the way they had been tackling it and said, "That will see me out." (It was like praying "Your kingdom come" and adding "but don't look to me to get involved"!)

We have had a great preaching tradition in Scotland, and it has been effective in giving people new eyes for living the truth. One in that tradition has been Stuart McWilliam. Just before his recent death, I asked him if he had anything to share, looking back on his life as a preacher. He replied simply, "We must start where people are." To invest life in creative change, to start right where people are, implies a revolution. Before our eyes in this day and age, we find SCCs living that way. We have concrete signs before us of what church may become.

In the Roman Catholic tradition, I noted earlier Bishop Patrick Kalilombe's reflection on the disturbance which may have to be faced by established hierarchies if laity were to be given their place (in accordance with Paul's word in Eph. 4:14,15 that members of the church are to be "no more children" but "fully grow up into Christ"). Juan Garcia Nieto, jailed under Franco, rejoiced that, as a result of his incarceration, the small community which had formed in the underground would need to shape itself in a priestless fashion. He spoke to me of the need for "conflictive faithfulness with the institutional church". In Rome, M. Vigli gave this testimony:

> I am a layman. In Italy, it is important to emphasize this because, until recently, lay people committed to the building up of the church have thereby been committed simply to being obedient. Those who did not obey either left the church or were marginalized by the church. The difference with the advent of basic Christian communities is that laymen have remained within the church and yet have taken up adult responsibilities for being church. This marked a clear break with the former tradition in which lay people accepted domestication – now, publicly, they insist on carrying their responsibilities.

So, what hinders?

At the root of what hinders in the church lies both unwillingness to give up power and unwillingness to take it. Clergy structures are unwilling to reverse the disinheritance of the laity; the laity, in turn, consent to and collude in that disinheritance. I am not referring to bare brutal power such as has been exercised by the church in past history. I mean the habit of those of us who are ordained of taking a leading role, the security of having a defined identity and a working agenda covering worship and pastoral care. I mean, also in turn, the cost in time and effort for lay people of adding to an already full working day what they need to "grow up fully into Christ".

It is no good for those of us who are clergy to complain, "I invite the membership to take a fuller part in the life and worship of the church, but they won't come forward." A tradition of disinheritance has to be overcome. It is no good for lay people to offer public prayers and scripture reflections if these are superficial, top-of-the-head stuff. The fact that they are laity does not itself qualify them. A whole job of re-equipping for a different form of church has to be undertaken. SCCs already put clergy and laity in a non-dominating relationship (note the experience of Paco on page 23), and help members to mature through mutual critical and supportive interaction, so that they learn to contribute effectively in worship and in life.

What, in the end, is the church meant to be like?

In first Corinthians 12 and Ephesians 4, Paul compares the church to a body. Jesus Christ is the head "from whom the whole body, joined and knit together by every ligament with which it is equipped, as each part is working properly, promotes the body's growth in building itself up in love". The upbuilding of the church to share in God's transforming purpose calls for the contribution of every member. For this purpose, a great variety of gifts of the Spirit are provided. There is no neck of clergy, whose role is to communicate the needs of the body to the head and the mind of the head to the body. We are simply part of the body. Other images for the church in the New Testament emphasize this togetherness: "household of God", "vine and branches", "bride of Christ", "shepherd and sheep", "God's building", "Christ's soldiers".

Here are some of the descriptions given by SCCs: "The people of God must be self-convened before the living-

Word-in-Christ without human masters." "The church is ordinary people trying to live the faith seriously and in freedom." "The sharing of life, goods, food, personal troubles and hopes, homes – all springing from the sharing of faith, Bible, eucharist." I find that one of my own reflections on the life-styles of SCCs describes them as "centred on Jesus Christ, teachable before the scriptures, given to prayer, nourished by worship, renewed in the sacraments, engaged in the world in kingdom struggles that justice and truth may prevail". They represent a renewed orthodoxy.

Wherever there is a sense that church, scriptures and sacraments have been alienated from the people, words such as "reappropriating" and "repossessing" may appear; and we may be reminded that ecclesiastical powers-that-be may concur enthusiastically in that recovery though it will take conversion from the old ways to effect this.

Gianni Novelli, a priest who worked as a sociologist, spoke of the contrast he saw between the attitude of church authorities to SCCs in Brazil and in Europe. A legacy of the 1964 coup d'état in Brazil had been the repression of democratic institutions. Hence:

> The church became the only point at which people could meet together to think and organize, so that even trade unions needed the churches in order to be able to develop their own work. Official trade unions were banned. What this meant was that people simply had to invent informal ways of organizing themselves to protest against the price of transport – or anything like that in the local situation that was preventing them from living their lives adequately. Probably more typical than bad transport was the lack of electricity. So there came into being emergent small communities attached to the churches, communities deeply concerned about and committed to the local problems they were facing. That was the real origin of the basic communities.

Effectively, what this meant was that the people repossessed the church. In this repossession, there were bishops and theologians who experienced what one bishop called a conversion. He rediscovered the church as the church of the people. One of the important things he discerned was that theologians became a means of liaison between the bishops and the people because they were circulating, they were keeping contact with both the hierarchy and the people in the grassroots development, and they did their theology among the people, not in separation from them.

This new role in the church of the theologian demanded the invention of a new name: *assessore*. The term was necessary simply to make it clear that there was now a different kind of theologian who was in full communication with the bishop and the hierarchy and in full communication with the people and working with the people.

There is a clear contrast with the European situation, where, quite often, the hierarchy sets its face against the Christian grassroots communities. Those bishops who had been converted to the cause of SCCs in Brazil saw to it that institutions and organizations of the church were organically related to the people's movement.

* * *

In the Philippines, Karl Gasper reflected on his experience, saying:

> The situation in Mindanao illustrates the importance of finding an authentic way for hierarchies and bureaucracies to relate to the grassroots of the churches... When the bishops cannot cope in the terms to which they have been accustomed, they are inclined to cut themselves off. This is illustrated by the Mindanao-Sulu pastoral conference [1971] where leadership emerged from outside the ranks of the bishops, that is, from those who could articulate the mind of the people and the direction which their faith ought to take in response to their situation. The bishops accused the conference of wanting a church without hierarchy, and when a new board was appointed, polarization increased.
>
> Are hierarchies necessary? Where there is co-responsibility of bishops with priests, nuns and laity, there can be a marvellously dynamic structure, where everyone is given respect and gains confidence. But different priorities will need to be accepted for the church because what is important is to build it

up, not to gain prestige. So bishops themselves must tackle the work of demythologizing their power roles. Hierarchy is still needed, but there must be a move from the form found in mediaeval Catholicism to a hierarchy which accompanies the people as they seek to find their role as Christians at this point in history (under threat of arrest, harassment and worse). Bishops must not allow themselves to absorb all the charisms and power of the people of God. Such an interpretation of their roles does not fit in with the collective leadership and decision-making which normally characterizes the basic Christian communities.

* * *

The experience of a Naples community shows the tension that can develop between Christians seeking new ways of living the faith and the traditional authorities:

The community took shape in the parish of St Gennaro in Vomero. Around 1968-70, a group began to meet to reflect on the will of God. The group was very aware of the way in which, through the gospel, the church could get more in touch with social reality. At the same time, lay people were beginning to make the word of God their own, sometimes with priests but not depending on them. The word of God, which had become the monopoly of clergy, was being reappropriated. The conviction of the members of the group that they had access to truth challenged the position of those who believed they were possessors of truth. The crunch came with the divorce referendum in 1974: they did not agree with the hierarchy's line.

The encouragement of people to vote according to their instructed conscience at the time of the divorce referendum was considered to be leftist. Franco, the parish priest, was pushed out of the parish, and others joined him.

The definitive founding of the community of St Gennaro in Vomero dates back to that time. The use of the name is partly a declaration that, although they have been pushed out, they want to be, and consider themselves to be, members of that parish. The group, with Franco as celebrant, held the eucharist in another church building. It was made a participative service. The sermon was no longer preached by Franco but built up by the community as a whole.

Once the parish at which they were guests fully understood what was happening, they refused them permission to meet on their premises any longer. Accordingly, they resorted once more to meeting and praying in their own houses, as the early Christians did. The group had had good relations with the Waldensian and Methodist community in Vomero, and now had access to premises which they made available. For the Roman Catholics, this was very important, this contact with other Christians. They now felt that, as Jesus had said that worship was not in Jerusalem, or "on this mountain", but "in spirit and in truth", they had begun to learn to worship in that kind of way as one Christian community. The bishop does not approve of this at all! It led to Franco's suspension. Now, in the eyes of the church authorities, we do not exist.

Words need to be matched by deeds

These recent examples come from the Roman Catholic tradition but similarities in other traditions will not escape the attentive reader. It will be noted that Karl Gasper speaks of hierarchies and bureaucracies together.

Of course the right noises may be made more often. Thus Pope Paul VI proclaimed:

> ...it belongs to the laymen, without waiting passively for orders and directives, to take the initiative freely and to infuse a Christian spirit into the mentality, customs, laws and structures of the community in which they live. Changes are necessary, basic reforms are indispensable; the laymen should strive resolutely to permeate them with the spirit of the gospel (*Populorum Progressio*, 1967, 81).

But when he issued *Humanae Vitae* in 1968, the promise represented by an advisory group of married couples, singles, women and men with competences which he, as a male, ordained, aged celibate lacked, was dashed when he went against their advice and forbade the use of contraceptives. The principle of subsidiarity, which declares that decisions in the church should be made at the appropriate level, had been ignored. When, as a matter of history, Paul VI's finding was put to the test, the principle of reception should have led the authorities to abandon it, for the faithful did not accept it in practice. The laity, though encouraged to be thinking, perceptive human beings, in the end were not trusted.

There is no sign of hierarchy in the apostolic and sub-apostolic ages – nor, we might say, of bureaucracy. It is a late development. We are into the 2nd century before the lineaments begin to appear. There begins a separation which gives a greater status to some of those who exercise forms of ministry designed to build up the church for its life in the world. It might have been understandable in light of circumstances at an earlier time. But it led to gradations of office which eventually laid claim to separate validation and effectively acted as if they were a neck between the Head and the body. Power connotations were added to functional assignments!

Separate development begins

Ignatius of Antioch (died c. 110 A.D.) came to the conclusion that a more disciplined form of government was needed. Wandering prophets, ostensibly bearers of information and resources for the strengthening of the small communities of Christians, could live off the land. In the *Didache* or "Teaching of the Twelve Apostles", believed to date from the late first or early 2nd century there is a warning in section XI about false prophets: "...whoever, in the Spirit, says 'Give me money or something else' you shall not hear him; but if for others in need he bids you give, let no one judge him..." This general guidance follows from the earlier admonition, "... when the apostle departs, let him take nothing except bread enough till he lodge again; but if he ask for money he is a false prophet." Section XV goes on "... now appoint for yourselves bishops and deacons worthy of the Lord, men meek and not avaricious and upright and proved; for they too render you the service of prophets and teachers."

In his seven letters to churches, written early in the 2nd century, Ignatius clearly had great difficulty in persuading them to accept such a change, even though at that time the emphasis remained on the communal working of bishops with presbytery and diaconate. But it may be that for his friend Polycarp, the monarchical bishop loomed on the horizon; in Polycarp's one extant letter, he continues to insist on communal oversight of the congregations.

What has developed, and resistance to it, may be observed today. Pope John Paul II, in consecrating an unusually large number of cardinals, called them "princes of the church". In contrast, Dom Helder Camara, bishop of Recife, Brazil, had pleaded with fellow bishops during Vatican II: "Let us end once and for all the impression of a bishop prince residing in a palace." He himself on arrival in Recife had replaced the gilded throne with a wooden chair and would not live in the palatial official residence but occupied a sparsely furnished room. Which of the two is nearer Jesus' warning against copying the styles of rulers of the gentiles and his commendation of servant power?

* * *

In different ways, the freeing of the laity to be church and live church demands the overcoming of forms of separation. Those forms are legitimate which cut off people from a variety of options in order that they may fulfil a particular mandate, as was the case with Barnabas and Paul in Acts 13:1–3. The problem is cut-offs which threaten Christian community, as when Paul took Peter to task for refusing to eat with gentile Christians. We will look at separation from commitments to engage in kingdom struggles, separation produced by intellectual demands, separation in equipping for ministry and that produced by the rite of ordination: in decision-making, in presiding at communion. We will also take into consideration the question of distinctive dress.

Engagements for kingdom objectives

Cardinal Ovando y Bravo in Nicaragua, with his declaration that good Christians do not engage in politics, is countered not only by the SCCs in Managua and Masaya but by Baptists in Rome. Nicaraguan SCCs who had taken part in the Nicaraguan revolution to an unprecedented extent saw the gains of that revolution being eroded – especially regarding education and health care for all – and set their faces against what they considered to be a threat to what were the signs of God's kingdom and righteousness. The Baptist pastor in Rome, whose flock had teamed up with Roman Catholics to form ecumenical SCCs, discovered that the revelation of God's will and purpose had to be related to situations which called for remedy if it were to be truly gospel. Reflecting on those who opted for either revelation or situation, not both, he produced the stunning saying, "We must never retreat into the Bible or retreat into politics."

Jesus did not come announcing church but kingdom – the whole fabric of created life being transformed so that it evidences God's mind and purpose in every part. This is to be sought actively in every age and is to be fulfilled in the city of God, where no church building exists because the church by then shall have fulfilled its assignment. How can the affairs of the world be neglected by believers who know that God so loved the world that he sent his Son...? Separation is justified only when its concern is to further God's purpose.

Intellectual demands

In the Western-dominated part of the world, intellectual demands are placed on those who seek to be ordained. But has intellectual attainment a definitive part to play in the building up of the church? I ask again that the observation of Schillebeeckx be given careful thought. He observed:

> If one places oneself in the perspective of the ancient church (the first thousand years) in terms of ecclesiology and ministry, then what one calls today a lack of priests will seem to derive from causes which are not linked to ministry itself. Notably, these causes are the conditions of admission to ministry which have been imposed during the course of history, for reasons which are not specifically ecclesiological. There are more than enough Christian women and men who possess the necessary charisma in terms of the theology of the church and ministry – such as, for example, many catechists in Africa, workers who are pastoral animators in Europe and elsewhere...: taking account of the canons of the ancient church, they match up to all requirements.

Delegates of the word, catechists, animators of various kinds – are not these gifted to enable the church to build itself up in love for the world? In our Reformed tradition in the West, the pattern of the one-man/one-woman band is so dominant that when there seems to be a shortage of clergy (do we still have too many?) they are asked to race round several parishes; and such appointees as "readers" or non-stipendiary ministers fill in, without changing the old pattern.

The church will need scholars. But they will need to work in league with the people, for scholarship must be related to challenges in the world if it is to contribute to theology. It must become less of an individual and more of a communal activity, embracing those with scholarship skills together with those who are immersed in testing situations remote from desks and classrooms. Theology is essentially a lay activity – people are already in the world, engaged in the world's affairs. In the Orthodox tradition, theological educators may be lay. Those of us who are ordained have a right to do theology only if we are engaged where it matters. Systematic theology is not a construct of abstract propositions but a shimmer of changing light to be appreciated by all kinds of people, as is the *aurora borealis*.

Theological colleges must suffer a sea-change. They have not been geared to their appropriate constituency. In my time, in Scotland, they were for ordinands only. The training then could be more accurately described as "scholarly" rather than "theological". Scholarship is a contribution to theology, no more though also no less. The work of scholarship can be tackled behind desks and within walls. Not so theology. Theology requires people to draw upon God's revelation to light up concrete situations in the world so that they might be handled creatively. That implies giving thorough analytical attention to the situations along with the revelation.

A limited number of scholars will still be needed specializing in biblical, church and allied matters. But the main constituency must now be drawn from those in business, commerce and public services who may be released for a month at a time to learn how to bring faith insights to bear on issues that face them. Theology is a much-needed resource for managing daily life. That must now be the concentration point. Then "theological colleges" will justify their name.

Equipping

To separate selected people for a period of years breaks them away from the flow of life as others experience it. If trainees are sent back into life in situations which test them thoroughly, as others in these situations are being tested, that may offer some remedy. But this rarely happens. Why should the equipping not take place so that people remain fully in the flow of life? Bishop Patrick Kalilombe made the point in an address already noted to the School of Oriental and African Studies in May 1985:

> Who needs expensive training? It may simply prove a handicap, preventing people from appreciating the resources within their own cultures, the gifts of their own people, the methods of gaining knowledge and handling life which have been tried and trusted through centuries.

* * *

Here are my notes on a visit to the Chuloteca district of Honduras:

> The small outpost had a room large enough for fifty or sixty people. They turned up in twos or threes. There was an earth floor. Hens angled their heads to size up the risks and, with many starts and flutters, managed to get a few pickings among the people's feet. Pigs nosed their way in at the door, intelligently decided that feet meant kicks, and ventured no further. The hens' want of intelligence clearly made them the gainers. Eventually, the service started and was enthusiastically carried through by leaders and participants. The *delegada de la palabra* (delegate of the word), the assistant *delegada* and the catechist (who was responsible for teaching the children) were all women. Afterwards they told me of the training they received, one session per month, in a town within reasonable distance. People were thus not withdrawn from involvement in their local

communities but, over a period of time, were resourced and built up for the leadership to which the church had appointed them in these communities.

* * *

That similar equipping of the laity may be provided in the West and for whole congregations was my own experience when I was parish minister in Rosyth for twelve years.

The parish church of Rosyth was in a situation of breakdown when we arrived in 1948. I saw that the role of the kirk session (or board of elders) could prove formative in building up the congregation. Early on, I suggested that we start meetings with Bible study.

The response was anything but enthusiastic: "We might look at that one bonny day – next business!" However, I persisted. At last, grudgingly, it was agreed that we open with one quarter of an hour of Bible study. Then half of the session members turned up with apologies a quarter of an hour late. Bible study with the others was like drawing blood out of stone.

Frustration itself may be productive. At one point, a painter from the dockyard rose and said, "I'm fed up with this. It's neither one thing nor the other. I move that, for a year, we do half-an-hour's Bible study, and that we all turn up and take part. If it hasn't worked when the year is up, we kill it stone dead."

It was unanimously agreed. Elders became fascinated by the relevance of biblical texts to their daily life. They participated eagerly and did not notice when the year had passed. After about eighteen months the painter rose again: "At first I got this all wrong. Earlier, when I mentioned the possibility of Bible study to my wife she said, 'It's 11 o'clock before you're home as it is. With Bible study it will be midnight.' It hasn't been like that. Bible study affects the whole session agenda. Things we would once have spent half-an-hour on we now get rid of in half-a-minute. We have learned to concentrate on essentials. I move that, from now on, we have an hour's Bible study to start each meeting." This, too, was unanimously agreed. From that time on, the only problem was stopping them after the hour.

The elders became a biblically equipped avant garde, leading the congregation beyond their existing perspectives and ideas. So many young people pressed in that we had to establish four Bible classes to cope with them. An elder was made responsible for each. When I was elsewhere on a Sunday, the elders conducted the morning and evening services.

The biggest risk and the biggest reward was when the whole congregation was given the sermon to preach. For this to happen, there had to be a public concern which everyone felt keenly about – such as a threat to close the dockyard, or an outbreak of juvenile delinquency or sewage carried into a school by bad drainage while different authorities passed the buck. Whatever the issue, it raised deep questions about what life is for.

Relevant passages of scripture were given out about ten days beforehand. Throughout the community, small groups formed and neighbours were approached:

"You've got to help us think through what light the Bible throws on such-and-such a situation."

"But I'm a Roman Catholic!"

"We need Roman Catholics."

"But I'm an atheist!"

"Good. We're short of atheists. Come on."

On the Sundays in question, 130 to 140 folk would gather. After the first part of the worship, I would go to the centre of the communion table with two people on each side. Their job was to offer one sentence each, drawing from scripture what they thought might illuminate the situation facing the community. Then it was up to the congregation.

Unfailingly surprised at themselves, they rose to the occasion and built up the sermon from that point, maybe thirty or so contributing. There was no need to intervene except to draw the communal sermon to a close and round off the proceedings at the close of worship.

The discipline was quite remarkable. If one speaker went off at a tangent, the succeeding one would bring the others back on course. A congregational mind seemed to come into being to guide the development of the communal sermon.

The effect was rich beyond words, as people drew upon a great variety of experiences of life and related these to their wrestling with the scriptures.

It took three years of work to get the session converted to Bible study, seven years to get them equipped to conduct worship, ten years to get the congregation to produce the communal sermon. Hard work, all of it: but how rewarding!

* * *

There is a particular *gift of the poor* for getting to the heart of biblical texts. Marc Luyckx, in Brussels, reflected on his contacts with SCCs in Europe and Latin America and contrasted these with the usual approaches in Western churches:

> Both in Belgium and in Recife (Brazil) these groups go directly to the Bible, whereas we seem to need piles of books before we can start. Why do we who are rich need so much writing, so much reading before we get to the biblical point which poor people reach in one step? It makes me wonder what we are doing regarding understanding the faith in the West. The Brazilians would say that we need to become poor and live with a big question in our belly to do this direct theology.

Chris Smitzkamp of the Salland community in the Netherlands observed:

> Every time we go to the Bible we have to reckon with a thick layer over it of traditional and ideologically slanted interpretations.

Special gifts for interpretation now enrich the church's understanding. Women who may be black, poor, illiterate have a special resource of experience which resonates with so much in the Bible, especially the psalms and parables. They know what it means to lose one coin. One such woman in an Oporto group observed that Mary's virginity was not in her physical intactness but in her bearing a child who would not be her own to raise her way.

Again, while scholars might concentrate on the implications of Jesus' ministry to the lost sheep of the house of Israel, in the case of the woman who pestered him in the region of Tyre and Sidon (Matt. 15:21-28) poor, ill-educated folk rejoiced that a woman and a foreigner should have been God's vehicle in reminding him of wider dimensions of his mission. While scholars concentrated on Jesus' right to forgive sins in the story of the anointing in Luke 7:36-50, poor folk rejoiced at Jesus' tenderness to an immoral woman.

Equipping people for different ministries should be undertaken to honour and make use of their particular gifts.

* * *

SCCs have been initiated by ordained or lay members of churches. Religious sisters, deacons and deaconesses played significant parts. I was put in my place by one sister when I suggested that only the poor could equip the poor.

In the ecumenical team which worked with SCCs in the shanty-town community of Tondo in Manila in the Philippines, my contact was Sister Victricia, a Sister of the Holy Spirit. I challenged her concerning the effect produced by the mere existence of the team. "Whatever your intentions might be," I said, "you are bound to be a manipulating presence among the shanty-town dwellers. All of you are educated. You are not stuck for words. You have know-how; you can manage the system as the Tondo people cannot. How can poor people assume leadership roles as long as you are there?" She met my challenge head-on:

> You've got it all wrong. We have a responsibility to articulate the situation the Tondo people are in to the point where they develop their own awareness and can articulate it for themselves. Then we must shut up. We have also a responsibility for identifying and proposing changes which dwellers in this area may successfully tackle themselves. Once they get going, and are encouraged to find they can get things done, people like us must get out of their way and let them get on with it.

I persisted, asking for an example. Sister Victricia illustrated from a water pipe which served houses in a particular area.

You can ask the people why should it not go to the next five houses. It would be useless to get them to face the question why water is not provided for the whole community in that sector – that would be biting off more than they could chew, starting on the wrong scale. If they can be convinced that a case may be made for the water pipe going to five more houses, they approach the authorities. They then find themselves, almost tongue-tied, in a room with a carpet on the floor and a man sitting behind a desk. But as they present their claim, certain changes take place. They find that they do have a case. They find that they can present it, though it may be in a stumbling way. They find that the man behind the desk may show signs of being a bit scared of them! They gain confidence. They get to know the ropes. They tackle larger matters. What we have started becomes owned by them, becomes part of their own struggle – and they will learn to put us in our place when that proves necessary!

Sister Victricia's judgment was ratified a few years later when the shanty-town dwellers stood up to the Federal Republic of Germany and got their emissaries to withdraw a scheme for extension of the harbour facilities which would have meant bulldozing dwellings in the Tondo area. By this time, they were also putting the team in their place, affirming: "We would rather live with bad judgments which we ourselves make than good ones which you make for us."

* * *

For Sister Ruth Egar of the diocese of Adelaide, Australia, the matter was straightforward. A diocese was equipped for mission and service through the development of SCCs. I asked her whether the small groups are fundamental in the structure of the diocese.

I believe they are, because I can see nothing life-giving enough happening other than in small communities. I see people putting their energies into administering the parish, in a sense to try to keep it alive and working; but you can't keep a parish alive without the spirit, and the spirit of the people must be made captive to the Holy Spirit. I believe that can happen only by people coming together in small communities. There is no other way. As I see it, we stand on the brink of a choice between the death or the ongoingness of our church.

Ordination

Ordination has been loaded with a heavy ecclesiastical weight which the word itself does not justify. In Eastern Orthodox churches it is understood, rightly, to be a form of authorization, not the imprinting of an indelible character on a person. When, in older editions of the Bible, words are translated concerning Jesus' "ordaining" of disciples (John 15:16), the underlying Greek word simply implies "appointing" and the emphasis lies not on the person but on the fruit-bearing which is regarded as a result. Ordination has sometimes been looked on as if it provided separate status through some change in the being of the person ordained. It was perceptive of Jan Klimes, my interpreter when I interviewed the Czech bishop Fridolin, to interrupt, pointing out that I started questions with "Bishop Fridolin..." as if that implied he held some separate, honourable position. "He just has a job like the rest of us," observed Jan. A layman rightly understood ordination.

Though the heavy weight given to the word "ordination" theoretically does not apply in my own tradition, the idea of separate status exists in practice. That is specially the case when it comes to presiding at holy communion.

Over the first centuries, such presiding at the Lord's table was not related to ordination but to orderly and thoughtful appointment. It is likely that, in house churches, it would be the householder who would be trusted to preside. Even Ignatius of Antioch in the 2nd century, with all his enthusiasm for extracting an individual from the team of oversight to put him in charge, says, "Let that eucharist be considered valid which is under the bishop or *him to whom he commits it*." There is no requirement of ordination. Pope Leo the

Great, in the 5th century, simply ruled that the people should be trusted to decide who was to preside. When, for the first time in history, third-world and first-world theologians met in Geneva in 1983, they summed up their gathering in a communion service presided over by seven women. No one knew who among them was ordained and who was not. What we all knew was they were appointed in an orderly manner by as comprehensive a gathering of the universal church as was likely to assemble anywhere.*

The great shame is where people may be deprived of the sacrament because no ordained person is available. Such a situation is in flat contradiction to Jesus' demand, "Do this in memory of me."

The practice in small Christian communities is varied. Where a pastor or priest is available, she or he most often presides, the understanding being that this is done in the name and at the behest of the company present. At times a hostile hierarchy or bureaucracy will forbid an ordained person to preside. Then other measures will be taken. One finds a custom of appointing four people for something like three months who will be responsible for discerning the issues to be faced in meetings of the SCC and will prepare eucharists; who will then give way to another four, till all have taken part except for those who choose not to do so.

I can testify to the imagination and thoughtfulness invested in such services compared with eucharistic services where the presider reads from a set script. It is not unusual for the whole group together to say the prayer of consecration, the body of Christ present consecrating the body of Christ to be received through the elements. In our own Iona community family group, the presider may be a Quaker woman.

Ordination must radically be rethought. Yes, there is a need for ministries which build up the ministering church. But what will be their purpose? Surely, two things only are

---

* See the report of this sixth international conference of EATWOT, *Doing Theology in a Divided World*, Maryknoll NY, Orbis, 1985.

needed: to identify, release, mature and locate appropriately the variety of ministries provided by gifts of the Spirit in every congregation, and to relate local to wider developments so that which is off-beat in a bad sense may be eliminated and that which is innovative in a good sense may be shared.

This implies a sea-change for selection and training committees, much more reliance on part-time dispersed learning courses such as the Scottish churches open college and much less dependence on traditional theological colleges.

Leadership and decision-making

In the SCCs, leadership emerges, and changes as different challenges are faced, and decisions are arrived at by way of group consensus.

Is consensus always possible? The Emmaus rural community, near Turin, was pressed hard on the matter:

> We do not want to develop a hierarchy, so we make decisions about what has to be done in common. Then, according to people's different gifts, the decisions are sorted into particular tasks. People in the area keep asking who our leader is, and we keep insisting that we do not have a leader. In the history of the group, wherever the community has tried to adopt a traditional leadership pattern, it has gone back. When people have struggled through to decisions they have made in common, the community has grown and matured.

What happened when they could not come to an agreed decision? "We keep talking through until we come to an agreed decision!"

But what if they were honestly divided and could not come to a common mind?

> Well, we just take time to go away and think things through again... Why should it not be humanly possible to have the kind of unity in a community which allows a common mind to develop and common decisions to be made? There is a difference between unity and uniformity. Each of us has a measure of independence. We are not made in the same mould. But we are, by choice, journeying together!

* * *

With hierarchies and bureaucracies the decision-making process often takes place far removed from grassroots realities. The small communities provide a sign that this is detrimental to understanding the church as a body in which different limbs and organs contribute to the life of all. In Wurzburg, the *Teestubengemeinde* testified:

> Our goal is that almost everybody be involved in the decision-making process. We try to have decisions at the lowest level possible; so every organizational team, like the peace team, the outreach or third-world team, is responsible for their own work and they take decisions concerning it. Then we have a leadership group of five people, and the five people consist of one from every group. They meet once a week and prepare the decision process. Very important decisions are discussed in the community meeting with everybody present, so that everybody may say what he or she is thinking about the decision, and the decision is made by all. But the leadership team has a more pastoral function, preparing decisions or deciding what themes we should discuss with one another, deciding what is important to speak about with one another. But everybody can come and say "please can we change this?", so there is an interaction between leadership and community.

* * *

In Australia, representatives of several home churches were interviewed together. The contribution of one member concerning leadership provided an experience clearly echoed in that of others present:

> It is not authoritarian or patriarchal at all. There is opportunity for everybody to take a lead where they feel able and are gifted for it. We do have, every six weeks, meetings of representatives from each of the groups to try to have a pastoral concern for the well-being of the groups as a whole, and that could be seen as an exercise of leadership in the total network. Though we make sure there's a representative from each group, any other member may attend. It is as leadership abilities emerge that people are given and take responsibility within the group.

Did the whole community take responsibility for its life and worship – and in the process, did particular members emerge as having the gifts and maturity that were wanted for particular jobs?

> Yes, that's right, and decisions are always made by the group as a whole. We wait until we can get consensus.

* * *

Jesus said, "One is your master, the Christ. You are all students" (Matt. 23:8-10). Leadership in the church has so often had trappings attached which elevate the one holding office. We have noted earlier that Bishop Patrick Kalilombe, speaking of BCCs in Africa at the School of Oriental and African Studies in 1985, pointed out the irrelevance of much that was exported from churches in the West to other parts of the world. He hazarded that the larger proportion of finance injected into churches in many African countries from rich churches in the West had no relevance other than a negative one to the style of life and Christian witness of the recipients.

A Czech bishop, active in the "silent" underground church during the communist regime, would wear no distinctive dress, would work for his living like others ("how can you serve people effectively if you are in a privileged situation?"), would conduct services in homes and workshops in preference to cathedrals. Jesus said of the vine-dresser, "Every branch which bears fruit he prunes that it may bear more fruit." The Czechs found that they were pruned back to essentials, and then recognized that to be a gift of God in spite of the raw experience they had to suffer.

Dress itself makes a theological statement. It may be argued that it performs merely a functional role. That may be the case in a hospital where, in an emergency, roles have to be explicit. But normally it extracts particular people, separates them from others, makes a distinction which tells against the unity of the body of Christ. In contrast, see Pedro Casaldáliga walking down a street in his open-necked shirt. No one will recognize him as a bishop. But his spiritual quality and openness to people is so evident that, if a passerby had some need, he, in the whole street, would be the one to be turned to.

In an indigenous congregation in Guatemala I asked who people would turn to in a crisis. I was told that no newcomer such as I was would be able to identify such a person. He or she might well be a quiet, nondescript person who took no leading part in debates. But if the people were at some crossroads, they would come to him or her, sit round, and be given the guidance which they themselves could then affirm from their hearts.

Responsibilities sometimes attach themselves to an office which are not in the compass of the bearer of the office. Chairing is a gift, an art, a skill. Moderators, superintendents, bishops often assume chairing responsibilities for which they have no competence. The late archbishop of Canterbury Michael Ramsey was as fine a Christian as you could ever come across. Because of his position, he was made chairman of the British Council of Churches. I never saw him actually chair one meeting. He would beam on the assembly and then retire into some inner chamber of the mind from which he would emerge occasionally to wag a finger or pat a head. But to bring an item of business to a conclusion, ensuring that everyone was given voice who should be heard, was not in his nature.

It is widely recognized in the world that there are ceremonies for which special dress is appropriate. The church is no different from other institutions. The best theological statement I have come across in this regard was in the Guatemalan community mentioned above (where SCCs were just getting started). The leader of worship entered with his robes over his arms. He put them on in front of the congregation. At the end of the worship (including a dialogue sermon), he took them off in front of the congregation and went out in normal clothes. A statement was thus made that assignments are given to certain people which may be recognized in a certain way, but that does not make them different from others who together make up the body of Christ.

Worship

When worship in the early church is described in First Corinthians 14:26-33 it is fully participatory, and developed in a way which is not marked by set responses.

Paul starts his description with the word *hotan*, "*when-ever* you gather...", in recognition that what he will describe is normal practice. He affirms the contribution to the building up of worship which comes from the gifts of the Spirit distributed among the people: "each one of you has a hymn, some instruction, a revelation, an ecstatic utterance or an interpretation"; later on, he affirms that all may give testimony, one at a time. He encourages members to distinguish between what should be contributed in a public assembly and what should be kept for sharing with God alone.

Now, we are not meant to be clones of the early church. Jesus said, "...the one who believes in me will also do the works that I do and, in fact, will do greater works than these, because I am going to the Father." All the same, we must give attention to that which developed when Jesus' earthly life was still a fresh memory.

I believe there are forms of worship which are different from First Corinthians 14 which can still claim authenticity:

a) A strong liturgy which contains all the elements of worship, where people know where they are and what is coming, may be apposite. Recently, a woman said to me, "Why do I continue going to church when the leadership of worship is dismal? It is because there is enough in the liturgy for me to invest in that!"

b) Worship which invades heaven and joins the adoration around the throne, such as you find in Orthodoxy, has an important place.

c) Single-voice leading which has freshness in prayers and sermon has its part to play.

Even so, the dynamic development depicted in First Corinthians 14 is missing almost everywhere in Britain today. Yet participation vitalizes and nourishes the life of SCCs. People grow and mature because they contribute to the building of worship, and in that participation share with others the problems and joys they experience in seeking to live out the faith in daily life.

So often the laity are not trusted to contribute significantly. Energy and effort are not put into their equipping. Note that Paul did not seek to douse down the dynamic nature of Corinthian worship. His one plea was for orderly development. Here is another word from a community in central Europe:

> The worship is prepared by lay people. We have a worship team, and this worship team selects the texts of the acts of worship – for example, we focus now at the time of the passion, using texts dealing with the cross. Then we have small groups in our community. Every small group takes one text and takes responsibility for one part of the worship, and they prepare the text or think what we can do with the text together; but the worship is celebrated so that everyone may participate, pray, ask questions and make comments on the text. The worship is so prepared that people can interact with one another.

* * *

Portuguese communities emerged from the experience of dictatorship, Czech communities from the communist occupation. There was a commonality, across so much of Europe, and yet, such different histories in the ways participant worship was developed.

In Oporto, Portugal, the service which mustered the small basic Christian communities in that area for a monthly celebration lasted from 10 in the morning to 5 in the afternoon. The first twenty minutes or so were spent in members hugging one another, exchanging greetings, and getting up to date with news. This was all part of the worship. The first hymn was one composed in the community. It was not only sung but danced. Bible readings followed. Then about an hour's sermon/reflection was built up from these. The small groups had met during the previous week and struggled to see how insights from the text could illuminate their life in the world. There was a mature interpretation. In the early afternoon, all shared a common meal – very much a feature of the worship of basic Christian communities. Mario, the worker-priest, then prepared the eucharist. The theological maturity of the communities' understanding of the eucharist is illustrated by Mario:

> It is the community who appoint the one to preside at the eucharist, and with a certain reluctance, I have accepted their invitation. I say reluctance because the priest is an equal with all the others in the celebration and speaks only when the others give him voice. He must always be attentive to criticism in the way he plays his part.

All this sounds too good to be true. But are these people "spiritual athletes"? Anything but. Listen to them when, the bread broken and the wine poured out, they tell of their own brokenness and pour out their hearts in union with the bread and wine. You will hear of frustration and failure in relationships affecting husbands, wives, young people, parents. You will be told of illnesses and despondencies. There will be word of humiliations and stresses at work, in searching for work, in looking for alternative work. "Cast down, but not destroyed" – the words come instinctively to mind.

The theme for the day is, "How are we to live the joy of our faith?" Sorrows shared, testimonies are made to a power which overcomes in and through suffering.

Members of the community do not depart until they have consolidated plans for the political and social engagements to which faith directs them. Some of these they will fulfil together, some separately.

* * *

Bishops may agree to preside, and may make that presiding a freeing of laity to build up the worship. Herewith my notes on a Czech visit:

> The last mass I attended before departure went this way. Bishop Fridolin presided, the other bishop at his side. The adolescents formed a band to lead hymn-singing. A time of confession was announced, and about half of the forty people present offered prayers. About the same number were later to contribute inter-

cessions. There was a responsive psalm. Bible readings came from members of the congregation. The New Testament text was the responsibility of an 18-year-old girl who proceeded to give the sermon. The children, who had gone out for their own sermon-equivalent, rejoined the company for the communion. They brought the elements and the vessels to the table and removed them at the end. The bishops together gave the blessing.

The service had the dynamic of First Corinthians 14:26–33!

8. The Form of the Church to Come?

Jesus said to his disciples, "Blessed are your eyes, for they see, and your ears, for they hear" (Matt. 13:16). He set this in contrast to eyes and ears closed against the challenge he represented. He urged his followers to be alert and awake to see and hear what God was doing in the world.

A similar call to remain alert is sounded for us in our day.

In four volumes entitled *Love in Practice: The Gospel in Solentiname*,* the priest and poet Ernesto Cardenal shares the perceptive comments of poor people who gathered in a small Christian community on an archipelago of Lake Nicaragua. They illustrate the capacity of ill-educated and illiterate people to get to the heart of the gospel and to perceive how it illuminates life. He gives credit, in his introduction, to the insights of different members. He then asks about the source from which they draw these insights. He concludes that "the true author is the Spirit that has inspired these commentaries (the Solentiname *campesinos* know very well that it is the Spirit that makes them speak)" and that "it was the Spirit who inspired the gospels".

What are we to make of the great proliferation of small Christian communities across the globe in our time? Are they a work of the Holy Spirit? If they are, eyes and ears must be alert to recognize in them a demand and promise for the future of the church.

- Some such phenomenon appears in the shaping and reshaping of church throughout Christian history. A need keeps declaring itself for small and intimate groups in which the demand and promise of the gospel may more closely be addressed and implications followed through.
- Take the early church. Members met in small companies in houses. These communities exhibited a great variety of life-styles, yet they were held together in a profound unity by the Holy Spirit.
- Take John Wesley's experience at the dawn of Methodism. That Christians "might help one another to work out their salvation", class meetings were established, and

---

* London, Search, and Maryknoll NY, Orbis, 1982.

later there came into being even smaller groups which Wesley called "bands". These comprised those who wanted to go deeper still into matters of faith and life. The effect was not to disrupt or divide the church but to nourish it.

- The recent survey of small Christian communities in the Roman Catholic tradition in the USA, funded by the Lilly Endowment, discovered that the average size of the SCCs was thirteen members – near enough to Jesus' twelve! In that size of group, devalued and shy people can find confidence, gain voice, enjoy growth.

The lives of SCC members are marked by orthodox belief. The risks they take are risks of faith. They provide a sign that the church is called to be a communion of communities with Jesus Christ and the kingdom of God at the centre, the church being ancillary. They release into leadership those gifted for it, including women and children. They welcome the ordained as part of the company without giving them the last word. They are nourished by the Bible, prayer and sacraments. They tackle theological tasks, recognizing that the untutored and illiterate may have deep insight into the mind of God, as Jesus affirmed when he set his theology in parables that still test the perceptiveness of educated and uneducated alike. In order to transform life towards the kingdom of justice and peace, SCCs are to be engaged in the world where it matters.

It follows that the validity of SCCs is not to be judged by their ability to fit smoothly into existing church structures. They provide a prophetic challenge to whatever in the church does not ring true to the gospel. Bishop Patrick Kalilombe has pointed out two equal dangers: that SCCs may be rejected out of hand, the traditional church's eyes and ears closed to their prophetic testimony; or alternatively, that SCCs may be treated by the church as unthreatening reinforcements, as if they were an extra engine added to the church train while it continues down the same tracks as before. Where dynamic interplay is set up between SCCs and the local parish organization, there can be mutual enrichment. It was so in Iglesia la Merced in Nicaragua. The seven SCCs that make up that parish met during the week, contributed prayers and built up the sermon communally on the Sunday, and then they each returned to their local gatherings with a larger vision.

It is time to ask afresh whether there is a dimension missing in the church wherever one fails to find some equivalent to that of small cells in a body. Ephesians 4:15-16 speaks about Jesus Christ "from whom the whole body, joined and knit together by every ligament with which it is equipped, as each part is working properly, promotes the body's growth in building itself up in love". The body of Christ under the direction of the head "builds itself up". This is not the creation of hierarchy or bureaucracy but of a multiplicity of functioning parts which supply energy and make growth possible. Then limbs and organs can be active in the world, enabling the body of Christ to effect his transforming purpose.

It is from a great variety of life-styles, drawn together in unity, that the church may build itself up in love. The most sensitive work I know of is that of my friend and colleague Jim O'Halloran. He may sojourn in some part of Africa for, say, two months. When he returns to the Salesian House in Dublin, two dozen SCCs may be found to have sprouted in places he visited. Not one of them will have a "J.O'H." stamp upon it. Each small group will have been encouraged to shape its life according to its own indigenous perception of what should make up its life.

SCCs would not themselves say that they form a *necessary* part of the fabric of church life. They would advise simply, "Go where the Spirit leads." But their very existence raises this question: Where no basic cell-structure exists, is there a missing dimension in church life?

Features of the early church provide instruction for us today. One is the building up of worship through the participation of members using gifts of the Spirit distributed among them, as in First Corinthians 14. If worship is always done *for* people, how can members, drawing on their varied life-experience, "grow up in every way into him who is the head" (Eph. 4:15)? How can they contribute to the building up of the whole Christian community? How can they mature in the exercise of ministries which together make up the one ministry of Jesus Christ in the world? The people of God are meant to give "light to all in the house" (Matt. 5:15), not to be like a lamp placed under a basket!

There is a need to restore confidence that worship is the work of the whole people of God, yet laity may be as reluctant as clergy to find themselves assuming responsibility for the needed changes. Restoration of the people's worship will involve a new confidence and a new self-discipline. St Paul makes the latter clear in First Corinthians 14:30-32: "If a revelation is made to someone else sitting nearby, let the first person be silent. For you can all prophesy one by one, so that all may learn and all be encouraged. And the spirits of prophets are subject to the prophets." It is not just participation that is needed, but thoughtful and disciplined participation, sensitive to when it is time to speak and when to be silent. This aptitude is best acquired in small companies where encouragement and criticism may be given without offence among people who have learned to trust one another.

In the worship and service of the church, it is necessary to give appropriate weight to local and to larger issues. The key is starting right where people are. The experience of Baptists in Rome is instructive. When they linked up with Roman Catholics to make ecumenical teams, their new colleagues alerted them to the plight of homeless people in their area. They did what they could to provide support. But in time, they became aware that the situation was not a matter of individuals falling through a net. There was a *systemic* problem of homelessness. It called for investigation of the structures of society, and this in turn led to a critique of the priorities of the city council. "To be obedient," said the Baptist pastor, "we Baptists had to get into city politics!" This led to a far deeper appreciation of the nature of structural poverty in the world (biblically, the poor are those *made* poor). In the process of addressing the social and political realities, Baptists and Roman Catholics together discovered that the Bible came alive for them as never before.

SCCs, coming into being right where people are, provide the disinherited poor with fresh hope and a place of belonging. They make possible nothing less than spiritual liberation. So often, members of devalued groups have been brought up to assume that the Bible and faith were only for the educated; meanwhile, they thought themselves lucky if they got crumbs that fell under the table. Given direct access to the Bible, they discover that it is in fact *their* book. It is all about farming and fishing, work in the house and fields, the disasters of a lost coin, a mugged traveller, conscripted labour and so on. The freeing of the Bible into the hands of the poor, who provide angles of interpretation "from the underside of history", enriches the whole church. Scholars have their rightful place. But scholarship is one contribution to theology, not theology itself. It must always be exposed to the test of real-life experience.

If the limitations of particular forms of knowledge and experience are to be overcome, the theological community must come to include the whole range of life experience represented within the people of God.

Although we are called to learn from the example of early Christian communities, contemporary churches are not asked to be clones of the early church. Jesus said "greater works than these [shall you do] because I am going to the Father" (John 14:12). He frees us to build on the foundations he laid.

In assessing the significance of small Christian communities in our time, the words of Gamaliel to the leaders of Israel are apt (Acts 5:35-39). Concerning the impact being made by the young church as it emerged from the strictures of Hebrew tradition that had nourished it, Gamaliel warned, "... if this plan or this undertaking is of human origin, it will fail; but if it is of God, you will not be able to overthrow them – in that case you may even be found fighting against God!"